GRACE, THE POWER OF THE GOSPEL

It's Not What You Do,
But What Jesus Did

by

Andrew Wommack

Harrison House
Tulsa, Oklahoma

Unless otherwise indicated, all Scripture quotations are taken from the *King James Version* of the Bible.

The author has emphasized some words in Scripture quotations in italicized type.

12 11 10 09 08 07   10 9 8 7 6 5 4 3 2 1

Grace, the Power of the Gospel:
It's Not What You Do, But What Jesus Did
ISBN 13: 978-1-57794-921-3
ISBN 10: 1-57794-921-8
Copyright © 2007 by Andrew Wommack Ministries, Inc.
P.O. Box 3333
Colorado Springs, CO 80934-3333

Published by Harrison House Publishers
P.O. Box 35035
Tulsa, Oklahoma 74153
www.harrisonhouse.com

Contents

Introduction

The book of Romans is the Apostle Paul's masterpiece. Punctuated with Old Testament examples, it's a detailed and scholarly treatise on the subject of grace. If you truly understand and receive its message, you'll be thoroughly convinced that right standing with God comes by grace, not your works.

Romans has literally changed the world. Back in the 1500s, Martin Luther became frustrated with all of his religious observances. When he finally despaired of ever earning his salvation, the Lord spoke to him through this verse in Romans:

> *Therefore we conclude that a man is justified by faith without the deeds of the law.*
>
> Romans 3:28

This spark of revelation not only changed Luther's life, but also ignited what we now call the Reformation. Its impact on individuals and governments literally changed the world—and continues to do so today.

Prepare to plumb the depths of God's grace!

Every revival has had a revelation of God's grace. Each awakening has possessed an acute awareness of man's need to forsake independence and acknowledge his dependence on God. Therefore, anyone desiring revival today must start with recognizing their own complete inability to produce right relationship with God through human effort and good works—both in the initial born-again experience and in day-to-day maintenance. The book of Romans deals directly with this same self-reliant, self-dependent attitude that still pervades the world. That is why Romans remains as timely for us today as when it was first written.

Through this brief synopsis of the book of Romans, the foundational truths of the Gospel burst into plain view. Prepare to plumb the depths of God's grace!

CHAPTER 1

Good News!

Paul wrote the book of Romans as a letter to the Christians in Rome. These Roman believers were mostly Gentiles who had received the Gospel, been born again, and were committed to following the Lord. However, they were being troubled by Jewish believers who were trying to mix the Old Testament law with Christianity.

In the early days of the church, many born-again Jews truly believed that Christianity was simply an extension of Judaism. Therefore, they considered all of the basic tenets of the Jewish faith—specifically the Old Testament law, the dietary regulations, the rite of circumcision, and many other Jewish religious observances—to still be the foundation of their new faith in Christ. They were trying to mix the Old Covenant with the New.

Paul—the apostle of grace to the Gentiles—boldly proclaimed that circumcision and all other adherences to Jewish custom and law were not necessary for salvation. His constant

> **Anybody who truly understands and embraces the message of Romans will be forever changed in the way they relate to God.**

struggle with legalistic Jews (called *Judaizers*[1]) is well documented in the book of Acts.

Although written for the same purpose as Romans, Paul's letter to the Galatians contains several strong, harsh rebukes against legalism. He started out by saying, "If anyone preaches any other Gospel than what I preached, let them be accursed!" (Gal. 1:8, *author's paraphrase*.) Then he repeated himself for emphasis. (v .9.) Paul also called the Galatians "foolish" and "bewitched" (Gal. 3:1) for believing this legalistic lie, telling them that if they were trusting in such things as circumcision for their salvation (Gal. 5:3), they had fallen from grace.

> *Christ is become of no effect unto you, whosoever of you are justified by the law; ye are fallen from grace.*
>
> Galatians 5:4

Romans presents these same truths, but from more of a doctrinal standpoint.

Whoever wrote Hebrews—I tend to believe it was Paul—also dealt with these very same things. Written specifically to a religious Jewish mindset, the book of Hebrews argues faith in the finished work of Christ using Jewish tradition (the Old Testament patriarchs, tabernacle, priesthood, sacrificial systems, among others) and showing how Jesus perfectly fulfilled it all.

Romans expounds the grace of the Lord Jesus Christ to both Jewish and Gentile believers. It's written to everyone! Anybody who truly understands and embraces its message will be forever changed in the way they relate to God. The revelation of God's grace contained in Romans delivers believers from a performance mentality—which bases relationship with God on our own efforts—to a total trust and reliance upon the Lord, His goodness, and grace. Salvation is all about God's faithfulness—not ours!

This revelation is foundational for maintaining a close relationship with God. We might do good for a while, but the truth is that all of us have sinned and fall short of His glory. (Rom. 3:23.) We need a Savior! We must constantly place our faith in God's goodness, and not our own.

> Many things that aren't good news have been promoted as "the Gospel."

The Gospel

Paul opened the letter with salutations and greetings. He commended the believers in Rome for how their faith was being spoken of throughout the world. Then, after expressing his desire to visit them, he summarized the message of the entire book:

> *I am not ashamed of the gospel of Christ: for it is the power of God unto salvation to every one that believeth; to the Jew first, and also to the Greek. For therein is the righteousness of God revealed from faith to faith: as it is written, The just shall live by faith.*
>
> Romans 1:16,17

> We don't have to atone for our own sin. We don't have to become holy enough to earn salvation.

The first five chapters of Romans communicate how the Gospel is the power of God. It's what produces the life of God in people.

Before we go into all of this, we need to define the word *gospel*. It's become a religious term that has actually lost a lot of its meaning today. Many people associate *gospel* with anything that has to do with religion—specifically the Christian religion. But the word *gospel* literally means "good tidings,"[2] or "good news."[3]

The Greek word *euaggelion*, which was translated "gospel" in seventy-four New Testament verses,[4] was so rare in writings outside of the New Testament that it's found only twice in the extra-biblical manuscripts we have access to. The reason for this is because this word not only meant "good news," but it was actually describing nearly-too-good-to-be-true news. There wasn't much in the world that was nearly too good to be true before Jesus came. But the biblical writers adopted this word because it was very descriptive of what the Lord did for us.

The Gospel is good news—not bad news! That definitely limits what we mean by the word *gospel*. Many things that aren't good news have been promoted as "the Gospel." For instance, quite a few people in the so-called "Christian culture" of the United States associate the Gospel with teaching that says, "You're a sinner. If you don't repent, you're going to hell!" Now, these are true statements. There is a heaven and a hell, a God and a devil, and you will go to hell if you don't repent and receive salvation. But even though all of that is truth, it's not good news.

A Free Gift

Many people have mistakenly thought that preaching on hell and scaring people out of it is the Gospel. That's not what Paul taught in Romans. As a matter of fact, as we dig deeper into this—showing the context and who the apostle was writing to—you'll see how that's the complete opposite of what he was really talking about. It's the goodness of God that leads us to repentance! (Rom. 2:4.)

Although it is true to tell someone that their sin has separated them from God and caused them to be worthy of eternal

| Nobody can save themselves. | damnation, the good news is that Jesus came and bore all of our sin for us. We don't have to atone for our own sin. We don't have to become holy enough to earn salvation. It's a gift. |

The wages of sin is death; but the gift of God is eternal life through Jesus Christ our Lord.

Romans 6:23

Most of religion today majors on the first part of that verse—"For the wages of sin is death"—and calls it the Gospel. They preach their hearts out about hell, fire, and damnation. I know. I grew up in one of those churches. People would literally grab the pew in front of them until their knuckles turned white. They'd feel such conviction and remorse. There is a place for that, but it's not the Gospel if all that's presented is God's wrath and judgment upon sin. The true Gospel specifically refers to the means by which we are saved. We're saved by faith in what Jesus did for us—not by faith in what we do for Him.

The Gospel is God's free gift of eternal life through Jesus Christ our Lord. The good news is that God doesn't want to send anyone to hell. You don't have to go through a tremendous amount of religious instruction or observance. It's a gift. All you must do is believe and receive. Believe what Jesus has done through His death, burial, and resurrection and receive the cleansing from all your sin and the freedom and liberty it brings. That's the Gospel!

God's Grace

The Gospel is directly related to the grace of God. That's the only way this forgiveness of our sins can be obtained. It wasn't through our holiness or good works. God doesn't take just the "good" people and save them. He justifies (extends salvation toward) the ungodly. (Rom. 4:5.)

This causes many problems for religious people. They say, "Wait a minute! I believe you must do this and that to be holy." Religion—false religion, man's concepts, not God-ordained salvation—teaches that right standing with God and blessings come as a result of our own goodness and works. It's always preaching, "You must come to this church. You must pay your tithes, do this, and do that. And if you do all these things, then God will accept you." That's anti-Gospel!

> If you're trying to be justified by anything other than faith in Christ, then you aren't believing the true Gospel."

It's against the good news of God's grace because it's putting the burden of salvation on your back—and you can't bear it. Nobody can save themselves.

That's basically the false "Gospel" that religion preaches today. They may even talk about the One true God and use terminology like "God the Father." They may even mention that Jesus is the Savior of the world who died for our sins. But at its core, it's another "Gospel"—which is no Gospel at all. (Gal. 1:6,7.)

In Galatians, Paul angrily rebuked this perversion of the good news. They didn't totally deny the foundational truths of the Gospel. They just perverted it and tried to add to it, saying, "Well, yes, Jesus is the Savior. But it's also based on your own goodness, holiness, and performance. It's Jesus plus you doing all of these things." Paul declared, "No, no, no—a thousand times no! If you're trying to be justified by anything other than faith in Christ, then you aren't believing the true Gospel."

The Gospel isn't only just belief that there is salvation, but it's also the specific method by which this salvation is obtained. "If you'll act good and do good, then you'll be good" isn't the true Gospel. Notice what Paul said while addressing the very first ministers' conference at Ephesus:

> *None of these things move me, neither count I my life dear unto myself, so that I might finish my course with joy, and the ministry, which I have received of the Lord Jesus, to testify **the gospel of the grace of God.***
>
> Acts 20:24

Another way Paul could have said this is, "I am testifying of the Gospel—which is the good news of the grace of God." In other words, the *Gospel* and *grace* are terms that can be used interchangeably. The good news—or Gospel—is the grace of God.

Grace Equals Gospel

Someone may say, "Well, I'm preaching the Gospel: God hates sin and He's angry at you. Repent or burn. Change your ways or you're in big trouble!" That's not the Gospel because it's not talking about the grace of God. Yes, there is a punishment for sin—but the Gospel emphasizes God's answer to it.

Paul also uses these two terms—the *Gospel* and *grace*—interchangeably in Galatians. Notice how "the grace of Christ" clearly implies the Gospel.

> *I marvel that ye are so soon removed from him that called you into the **grace of Christ** unto another gospel.*
>
> Galatians 1:6

Galatians was written for the same reason as Romans—to establish the grace of God.

The Gospel is good news. It specifically refers to what Jesus did for us. It's based upon His performance, not ours. Our good works and "holiness" do not earn us salvation. We must get away from this dependence on self. It's sad to say, but much of what is called the Gospel today is actually promoting trust in self rather than trust in the Savior. That's just false religion!

The Only Way to Salvation

Grace is what sets true Christianity apart from every other religion in the world. Other religions may acknowledge and worship a "one true God." They may even agree that Jesus existed and that His teachings are admirable. They say that He was a good man, perhaps even a prophet, but definitely not God manifest in the flesh. Religion refuses to acknowledge Jesus Christ as the only way to salvation—right relationship with God.

Every false religion—even religious Christianity—puts the burden of salvation upon the individual. In other words, "salvation" is based upon your performance. If you live holy enough, do enough good things, observe all of these rituals and rules, then you might be able to be saved. The problem is—and Romans makes it crystal clear—that none of us can live up to those standards. We can't save ourselves!

> The Gospel—as referred to in Romans—speaks of the good news of salvation independent of our performance.

True Christianity is the only faith on the face of the earth that has a Savior. On Judgment Day, each one of us must stand alone before God and answer the question, "What makes you worthy to enter into My presence?" The followers of every other religion will say, "I was holy and gave to the poor. I never did these things and always did these others. I even journeyed to the holy city and performed the prescribed rituals. I prayed three times a day, and fasted." However, the Word plainly reveals that all have sinned and fall short of God's glory. (Rom. 3:23.) Who wants to be the best sinner that ever went to hell? Therefore, you simply cannot trust in yourself for salvation.

However, a born-again believer would answer that same question differently. They'd say, "Jesus Christ is my Lord and Savior. I'm trusting completely in His goodness and His performance. It's definitely not anything I've done. I get in based on what He did for me through His death, burial, and resurrection." Now that's the right approach!

Independent of Our Performance

Many people around the world who have embraced "Christianity" have never heard the true Gospel preached concerning God's goodness and grace. They're simply substituting "Christian" things to do instead of Muslim, Hindu, Buddhist, or some other religion's things to do. To many people, Christianity is nothing but a different set of rules, doctrines, and regulations whereby they must earn their way to God. That's not the true Gospel—and it's exactly what the book of Romans confronts.

The Gospel—as referred to in Romans—speaks of the good news of salvation independent of our performance. It's by God's grace. That's nearly too good to be true. But it is. Thank You, Jesus!

CHAPTER 2

Without Excuse

This word—*salvation*—has become a religious cliché that many people associate with the initial born-again experience.

> *I am not ashamed of the gospel of Christ: for it is the power of God unto salvation to every one that believeth; to the Jew first, and also to the Greek.*

> Romans 1:16

Those who have been exposed to evangelical Christianity often believe that salvation is an experience—a one-time occurrence where you get your past sins forgiven. It continues on indefinitely, and we grow in it, but there's a definite beginning place—an experience where you pass from death to life. Although this is true, it's incomplete. Biblical salvation isn't limited only to this initial born-again experience where we get our sins forgiven.

A Package Deal

Salvation is everything Jesus purchased for us through the atonement. *Sozo*—the Greek word from which "salvation" was translated the vast majority of times in the New Testament—means more than just forgiveness of sins. It's also healing, deliverance, and prosperity.[1] *Sozo*—salvation—is an all-inclusive word that summarizes everything that Christ provided for us through His death, burial, and resurrection.

God is beyond being impugned in any way. He's perfect and faithful. All His promises are true.

Sozo was also applied to healing a number of times in the New Testament. James 5:14-15 vividly illustrates how salvation includes both healing and forgiveness of sins:

> *Is any sick among you? let him call for the elders of the church; and let them pray over him, anointing him with oil in the name of the Lord: And the prayer of faith shall save* [sozo] *the sick, and the Lord shall raise him up; and if he have committed sins, they shall be forgiven him.*

Salvation is a package deal. It's not only forgiveness of sins, but it also includes healing, deliverance, and prosperity. Therefore, when the Scripture says that the Gospel is the power of God unto salvation, it's not just talking about how to be born again and have your sins forgiven. It also means that the

Gospel—the grace of God—is the power of God unto healing, unto deliverance, unto prosperity—unto everything that comes to us as a result of being born again. It's talking about your relationship with God.

Do you need to be healed? The power for healing is in the Gospel. Do you need to be prospered financially? The power for financial prosperity is in the Gospel. Do you need to be delivered from the power of demonic influence, from depression, from yourself, or from something else? The power for deliverance is in the Gospel!

Satan's Biggest Weapon

You might be thinking, *But I've heard the Gospel and I still need healing in my body.* I don't believe we've truly understood the Gospel. It's more than just understanding *that* Jesus came to the earth to set us free. It's also understanding *how* God set us free through Jesus coming to the earth. It's how we relate to God based on grace (what Jesus did) instead of performance (what we do).

Satan tries to get us to earn the things of God, to make ourselves our savior, to put our faith in what we've done instead of

> Most people believe that God moves in their lives proportional to their performance.

faith in Christ as our only means of receiving from God. This is his biggest weapon against us!

The devil cannot effectively discredit God. Anyone who has had an encounter with the Lord, and has any sense at all, knows that God is beyond being impugned in any way. He's perfect and faithful. All His promises are true. It's not even an issue.

So instead of coming right out and telling people that God doesn't heal (prosper, deliver) today, Satan deceives them into thinking that they must do something in order to earn God's provision. This causes them to doubt the Lord's willingness to use His ability on their behalf. Instead of relating to and receiving from God based on His grace, goodness, and mercy, they try to earn God's gift through human effort. Can you see how this lie is contrary to the Gospel?

> "The Lord loves us in spite of who we are and what we've done."

I've had many people come up to me in prayer lines, asking, "Why aren't I healed? I've fasted, prayed, and studied the Word. I pay my tithes and go to church. I'm doing the best I can! What does God demand?" A person like that has just told me why they aren't healed. They didn't point to what Jesus did for them. They're pointing to what they've been doing for Jesus. Most people believe that God moves in their lives proportional to their performance. That's just not true!

This is what Paul was preaching against. He wrote this letter to a group of people who were being influenced by Jewish thought. This Jewish mindset was based on the concept that you had to keep the law, do all these things, and only if you were holy enough would God accept you. In other words, this was a religious system preaching: "God is God and you're a sinner. He's angry with you. Unless you repent, there will be no mercy for you!" It was a religious system of thought that used the preaching of God's wrath to turn people from sin through fear of punishment.

Then Paul came along and said, "I'm not ashamed of the Gospel!" This word *gospel* has become such a religious cliché that many who embrace it today don't even really know what it means. But in Paul's day, they knew exactly what he was saying. He was talking to people who were literally trying to scare the devil out of people through fear of wrath and punishment. That was their total approach to God. Into this mindset walked the apostle of grace, saying, "I'm not ashamed to tell people about the goodness, grace, and mercy of God. The Lord loves us in spite of who we are and what we've done." Now that's good news!

Intuitive Knowledge

Of course, the religious folks of Paul's day thought this was terrible. "What he's preaching is heresy! People need to recognize and relate to God based on how sorry they are. We are nothing but worms in His sight—no good!" This is really a deception. "God is angry with me. I have to improve and do all these things." Wrong! On the surface it looks like they're really turning from self, but in reality it's actually making that person's relationship with God dependent on themselves—how much they've done for the Lord, how holy they are, how much they've denied themselves, how good they are. This is actually a very self-centered, self-dependent way of approaching God.

Paul came along and talked about God's goodness and grace. He said to just receive by grace. It's the goodness of God that leads us to repentance. (Rom. 2:4.) The only way we can turn from self-reliance is by putting all of our faith, dependence, and hope in God's goodness, mercy, and grace.

It's the Gospel that has power in it. Our holiness and efforts to perform won't set us free from guilt and condemnation. We need to humble ourselves and say, "Father, I can't do it. I need a Savior. I come to You and throw myself upon Your goodness, mercy, and grace." That's what breaks the dominion of sin over us.

Since most people relate to God based on fear instead of love, no doubt the immediate response of those Paul was writing to would've been, "But you can't do this! People have to know how ungodly they are. How will they turn from their sin unless they understand God's wrath?" Paul answered this question by saying:

> *The wrath of God is revealed* [not going to be, but already is revealed] *from heaven against all ungodliness and*

unrighteousness of men, who hold the truth in unrighteous-
ness; because that which may be known of God is manifest in
them; for God hath [past tense] *shewed it unto them.*

Romans 1:18,19

God's wrath has already been revealed intuitively inside of
every person. Each individual has within them an intuitive knowledge of God's wrath against all ungodliness and unrighteousness
of men. So, when someone wonders, *If I just tell people about the*
goodness of God, what will make them understand that they are
sinners in need of salvation who need to turn from sin? Paul's
answer was that they already knew. In their hearts, people already
know that they aren't God, but sinners in need of salvation.

No Atheists in Foxholes

The invisible things of him from the creation of the world
are clearly seen, being understood by the things that are
made, even his eternal power and Godhead; so that they are
without excuse.

Romans 1:20

Even the people who have lived in the most remote parts of
the earth and have never had anyone preach the Gospel to them
will be accountable to God when they stand before Him
someday in eternity. Why? Because they had this intuitive
knowledge that there is a God and they're separated from Him

and in need of salvation. They'll be "without excuse." Many Old Testament scriptures agree.

I saw this truth vividly illustrated as a soldier in Vietnam. Outside of my brigade headquarters, there were three very old temples standing side by side. Since there was only about a foot between each of them, the three taken together appeared as one larger temple. At the time I saw them, trees were growing out of them and parts were falling down through the effects of weather and lack of use. When I asked about them, someone told me that these temples predated the introduction of Christianity to Vietnam by at least 500 years. However, these people worshiped a god that was manifest in three persons. This relates to what Christianity calls *the Trinity*. I'm not saying that these people worshiped the true God or that they had a true revelation of Him. But this does show this intuitive knowledge of the Godhead that Paul was referring to in verses 18-20.

Many of my fellow soldiers in Vietnam professed to be atheists. They tried to deny this knowledge in their hearts that they were sinners. One such fellow barged in on one of my Bible studies and ruined it. He threw lofty intellectual questions at me that I couldn't answer. He left laughing and took all the people with him. It looked like I was a total loser in that situation.

While he was grilling me, I kept saying, "I don't know the answers to all of these questions, but I know in my heart that God is real. And I know that you know in your heart that God

is real. You're just trying to deceive yourself." He kept answering, "Nope, there is
no God. I have no conviction, no awareness of God." He maintained that front all
the way out the door.

However, within thirty minutes he came
back into that chapel where I was sitting and
began to cry. Between tears, he blubbered, "I
want what you've got. I know there's a
God!" You see, when the bombs began
falling and the bullets started to fly, I'd hear
those same guys who called themselves
atheists scream out to God for mercy at the top of their lungs. The
old saying rings true: There are no atheists in foxholes!

> We don't need to convince people they are sinners and get them condemned. We need to show them the way out of the mess they're in.

Progressive Steps

What Paul said in Romans 1:18-20 is true. Every person has
this intuitive knowledge of God. Sure, they may get into some
type of mind game and try to sidestep it. But ultimately, the
truth is that this knowledge has indeed come to them.

For the rest of Romans, chapter 1, Paul began explaining
how these people—who have this intuitive knowledge of God's
wrath—end up living the way they do. It's a progression.

> *Because that, when they knew God* [this intuitive knowl-
> edge], *they glorified him not as God, neither were thankful;*

but became vain in their imaginations, and their foolish heart was darkened.

Romans 1:21

Their hearts became hardened toward the things of God. Then, from that point, there were progressive steps further away from Him. In their foolishness (v. 22) they worshiped animals (v. 23), dishonored their bodies (v. 24), and became idolaters (v. 25). Because of this God gave them up to "vile affections" (v. 26) and a "reprobate mind" (v. 28). The rest of Romans 1 shows progressive steps they took away from God.

The point is that you don't have to literally bombard people with their sin and the fact that they are a sinner on their way to hell. Deep in their hearts they already know it because of this intuitive knowledge. You may need to spend some time on that issue in order to make your point and strike that chord in their hearts, but not like the legalistic Jewish approach that condemned people and put many restrictions and bondages on them. Paul was saying, "That's not the true approach."

It's the Gospel—the nearly-too-good-to-be-true news that God has provided salvation for us by grace—that empowers men to receive the forgiveness of their sins, the healing of their bodies, the deliverance from Satan's oppression, and whatever else they need. We don't need to convince people they are sinners and get them condemned. They already know that and feel condemned. We need to show them the way out of the mess they're in. That's what the Gospel does!

CHAPTER 3

The Purpose of the Law

In Romans 2, Paul started going after these Jews who were trusting in all of their goodness, saying, "You're just as guilty as these other people. In addition to this intuitive knowledge that everyone has, you've also been given the law of God. Not only do you have an inner witness, but you also have an outer witness. Therefore, you're doubly guilty!"

> Despisest thou the riches of his goodness and forbearance and longsuffering; not knowing that the goodness of God leadeth thee to repentance?
>
> Romans 2:4

God's goodness is what causes people to repent—not His wrath. God's wrath may be able to get their attention, but it can't change their hearts. Only His goodness and mercy can do that.

> By mercy and truth iniquity is purged: and by the fear of the LORD men depart from evil.
>
> Proverbs 16:6

> Salvation is everything you need—forgiveness of sins, healing, deliverance, and prosperity.

The fear of God may cause someone to decrease the amount of their sin, but it can't purge them from iniquity. Mercy and truth are needed for that. An individual can actually be brought to the point of recognizing their need for salvation through the preaching of God's wrath and judgment. But it's powerless to change their life. God's goodness is what leads people to repentance.

Guilty!

This is what Paul dealt with in Romans 2. These Jews disdained these nonreligious people because they weren't keeping the rituals and holy standards of the law. They were pointing their fingers and saying, "There's no way you can be accepted by God!" Paul turned the tables and declared, "You're just making it worse on yourselves. Since you've been given a superior knowledge of God's right standards through the law in addition to your intuitive knowledge, you're doubly guilty! You now have a mental understanding of what is demanded of perfection, and you know you're not keeping it." The point of this, of course, was to shut their mouths.

Paul summarized all of this in chapter 3, saying, "It doesn't matter if you're a Jew or a Gentile, if you're religious or not—

everybody's guilty before God. The religious person doesn't really have an inside track. Religion doesn't make you any closer to God. It actually makes you more accountable—guilty—than the person who hasn't learned all of these right standards."

> *As it is written, There is none righteous, no, not one: There is none that understandeth, there is none that seeketh after God.*
>
> Romans 3:10,11

In context, the point Paul was making is that neither the unreligious nor the religious are able to stand before God. The non-religious can't claim total ignorance because of their intuitive knowledge, and the religious person can't claim acceptance and demand relationship with God because they are falling short of the very things that they know both mentally and intuitively.

The Law Is for Whom?

> *They are all gone out of the way, they are together become unprofitable; there is none that doeth good, no, not one.... Now we know that what things soever the law saith, it saith to them who are under the law: that every mouth may be stopped, and all the world may become guilty before God.*
>
> Romans 3:12,19

Paul has already said that it's the Gospel—the good news about God's grace and mercy—that produces salvation.

> Only the
> Gospel—
> the grace of
> our Lord Jesus
> Christ—can purge
> our sin away.

Salvation is everything you need—forgiveness of sins, healing, deliverance, and prosperity. It's a gift, not something you earn.

He's also shown that nonreligious people already have a knowledge of the wrath of God and that religious people are doubly guilty. We're all guilty before God. That's the point Paul just made. Then he came back to the religious person, specifically the Jewish nation, and said some startling things.

> *Now we know that what things soever the law saith, it saith to them who are under the law.*
>
> Romans 3:19

What a radical statement! Some people think that the law was given for everyone. No, the law was given to the religious Jew. It was a covenant between God and the Jews. The law was never intended for the Gentiles. The Jewish Christians were saying that the Gentile believers had to convert to Judaism and observe all of these laws before they could become Christians. Paul said that the law wasn't even given to the Gentiles.

Every Mouth Stopped

So what was the purpose of the law? According to the Apostle Paul, its purpose is completely opposite of what most people think. He revealed it to us in Romans 3, 4, and 5. In Romans 3 we're told that it was given unto those "who are under the law: that every mouth may be stopped, and all the world may become guilty before God" (v. 19).

The law was never given for the purpose of justification. That's what the Jews were saying, and it's what many people say today: "You must keep all the precepts of the Old Testament law. God judges you based on how well you perform." Not true! That wasn't its purpose.

> *Therefore by the deeds of the law there shall no flesh be justified in his sight: for by the law is the knowledge of sin.*
>
> Romans 3:20

The law wasn't given to produce salvation or the forgiveness of sins. Mercy and truth is what purges iniquity. (Prov. 16:6.) The knowledge of sin and the wrath of God may motivate people to limit the amount of their sin through fear, but it's completely incapable of ever forgiving or wiping that sin away. Only the Gospel—the grace of our Lord Jesus Christ—can purge our sin away.

According to Romans 3:19, the purpose of the law is to shut your mouth. In other words, the law takes away all of your excuses and comparisons. It gives you a knowledge of sin and makes you guilty before God.

Pointing to the Eternal One

Now the righteousness of God without the law is manifested.

Romans 3:21

Here's another radical statement. Paul was saying that the righteousness of God without the law is now manifested. In other words, you can become righteous, enjoy right standing with God—just as if you'd never sinned—and be completely forgiven, made clean and pure in God's sight, without keeping the law. This upsets religious people today just as much as it did in Paul's day.

But now the righteousness of God apart from the law is revealed, being witnessed by the Law and the Prophets.

Romans 3:21

All the Old Testament—the law and the prophets—pointed forward to this. They foreshadowed and prophesied it. People who take commandments in the Old Testament law and teach that you must do them to be accepted by God totally misunderstand its purpose. The law and the prophets testify to the coming of the Righteous One—the Lord Jesus Christ—and righteousness given as a free gift through faith in His name. The law was only a temporary thing that projected and prophesied the coming of the Eternal One.

I recognize that I'm covering a lot of ground quickly. For a more in-depth look at this, I encourage you to get hold of my teaching entitled *The True Nature of God.*[1]

Most people think that the law was given by God to show us all of the things we had to do to get right with Him. Wrong! That's not the purpose of the law. Remember, the law shuts our mouths by making us aware of our sin and guilt before God.

> The law didn't strengthen us in our battle against sin. It strengthened sin in its battle against us.

The Strength of Sin

What shall we say then? Is the law sin? God forbid. Nay, I had not known sin, but by the law: for I had not known lust, except the law had said, Thou shalt not covet. But sin, taking occasion by the commandment, wrought in me all manner of concupiscence. For without the law sin was dead. For I was alive without the law once: but when the commandment came, sin revived, and I died. And the commandment, which was ordained to life, I found to be unto death. For sin, taking occasion by the commandment, deceived me, and by it slew me.

Romans 7:7-11

The law made sin come alive. It revived the sin on the inside of us and gave it an opportunity against us.

The strength of sin is the law.

1 Corinthians 15:56

The law didn't strengthen us in our battle against sin. It strengthened sin in its battle against us.

This runs contrary to the way most people think of the law. They believe that the law was given to break sin's dominion over us. Not so!

Sin shall not have dominion over you: for ye are not under the law, but under grace.

Romans 6:14

If you're under the law, then sin has dominion over you. The law strengthens sin in its battle against us, not us in our battle against sin. Why?

Simply put, sin had already defeated us. Even if we kept ninety-nine out of a hundred commandments, that one we broke caused us to become guilty of everything.

Whosoever shall keep the whole law, and yet offend in one point, he is guilty of all.

James 2:10

In God's eyes, even the slightest sin contaminates us. He doesn't grade on a curve. He doesn't just take the people who are closer to keeping the law as better than others. It's all or nothing. Either you're perfect, or you need a Savior. Since no one can keep the law, sin had already defeated us. Those who were trying to overcome sin were fighting a losing battle because all have already sinned and fallen short of the glory of God. (Rom. 3:23.) There was no way to eradicate what had been done.

> God raised the bar so high through the law that no one can measure up. It was to show us that none of us can save ourselves.

Flat on Your Back

The law was given to bring us out of our deception that we could ever save ourselves. God revealed what real holiness is for those who think, *I'm close. I'm a pretty good person*. He gave a standard of holiness that was so detailed—step one through ten thousand—that it was impossible for anyone to ever keep it. The purpose of the law was to drive us to our knees, saying, "If this is what God demands, I can never keep it!" The law wasn't given so we could keep it. It was given to show us that we could never keep it. Once we're aware of this, we find ourselves shut up to the fact that we need a Savior. We realize that forgiveness and mercy is the only avenue on which we'll ever have right standing with God. That was the purpose of the law.

Imagine being in a large room with many people. If God walked in and said, "You must all jump up and touch the ceiling or die," what would you do? If the ceiling was only eight feet

> The righteousness that comes from God is perfect, holy, and infinitely greater than any righteousness we could ever obtain through our own efforts.

tall, you might be able to jump high enough to save yourself. But what if the ceiling was thirty feet tall? You might be able to jump higher than someone else, but if thirty feet was the minimum, you'd be doomed. All you could do is plead for mercy. Likewise, God raised the bar so high through the law that no one can measure up. It was to show us that none of us can save ourselves. We need a Savior!

The law was given to condemn you—to kill you (2 Cor. 3:6, 9), meaning that it's supposed to knock you flat on your back so that the only way you can look is up. Sad to say, religion has very subtly turned it around. It's encouraged people to embrace the law and try to keep it, thinking they can earn right standing with God. Impossible! That cannot happen. Paul was bringing this out in these passages of scripture.

> *Now the righteousness of God without the law is manifested, being witnessed by the law and the prophets; even the righteousness of God which is by faith of Jesus Christ unto all and upon all them that believe: for there is no difference.*
>
> Romans 3:21,22

Verse 22 emphasizes the righteousness of God. There are two kinds of righteousness (see Rom. 9:30-10:10). The righteousness that comes by living as best you can according to the law may benefit you in your relationships with other people and in limiting Satan's inroads into your life, but it's totally ineffective in achieving right standing with God. No matter how well you do, you're still far short of what the Lord intended and demands. But the righteousness that comes from God—a God-given righteousness—is perfect, holy, and infinitely greater than any righteousness we could ever obtain through our own efforts.

We're All in the Same Boat

All have sinned, and come short of the glory of God.

Romans 3:23

This scripture is often used to preach guilt and condemnation. The goal is to make people feel unworthy and recognize their need for God.

Let's consider this verse in context. Verse 22 just said that we receive "the righteousness of God which is by faith...unto all and upon all them that believe," speaking of both the religious and the nonreligious, the holy and the non-holy. It's a gift to both. In God's eyes there is no difference. It doesn't matter how religious or "holy" you are, everyone has sin in their life and comes short of His glory.

God's standard isn't me, somebody else, or some religious system. It's Jesus. And every one of us has come short of that standard. Nobody measures up to Jesus!

[We are] being justified freely by his grace through the redemption that is in Christ Jesus.

Romans 3:24

The emphasis here is that we're all in the same boat. We're all sinners and we've all been "justified freely by his grace through the redemption that is in Christ Jesus." This is powerful!

Justified by Faith

For the rest of the chapter, Paul summarized by saying, in essence, "It doesn't matter if you are better than somebody else. We've all sinned and come short of God's glory. Therefore, we all need to be freely justified. You can't claim that you're closer to God and need less of His grace than someone out there living a totally reprobate life. We all need the same thing. We all must come to God through the Lord Jesus Christ."

Therefore we conclude that a man is justified by faith without the deeds of the law.

Romans 3:28

1. What is the difference between our righteousness and the righteousness of God?

2. In your own terms, how would you describe what the statement "we're all in the same boat" means regarding the keeping of the law and grace?

CHAPTER 4

Faith Accesses Grace

*Do we then make void the law through faith? God forbid:
yea, we establish the law.*

Romans 3:31

Someone may ask, "Well then, why did God give all of
these commandments if salvation is just by grace?" Again, this
betrays a misunderstanding of the purpose of the law. They're
still thinking that God gave the law so we could keep it and
thereby earn relationship with Him. That's not the purpose at
all. In Romans 4, Paul went on to use examples from Scripture
to answer this question, beginning with Abraham.

*What shall we say then that Abraham our father, as
pertaining to the flesh, hath found?*

Romans 4:1

Some people believe that Abraham was justified by God
through his holy life. However, anyone who thinks this hasn't

carefully read the Scripture. Abraham had some serious problems in his life!

> *If Abraham were justified by works, he hath whereof to glory; but not before God. For what saith the scripture?* [Then Paul quoted Gen. 15:6.] *Abraham believed God, and it was counted unto him for righteousness. Now to him that worketh is the reward not reckoned of grace, but of debt. But to him that worketh not, but believeth on him that justifieth the ungodly, his faith is counted for righteousness.*
>
> Romans 4:2-5

God promised Abraham that seed would come out of his own bowels that would become as numerous as the stars in the sky and the dust of the earth, and in him all the nations of the earth would be blessed. (Gen. 12:2-3; 13:16; 15:4-5.) Abraham then believed God and the Lord counted him—at that moment—righteous. (Gen. 15:6; Rom. 4:3.) This was thirteen years before Abraham received the sign of circumcision, which is the dominant tradition these legalistic Jewish believers were trying to impose upon the Gentile Christians. Paul was showing how these things were proven even in the Old Testament. They were there for those who would read it.

God Wants Your Heart

Then he shifted his attention to David:

> *Even as David also describeth the blessedness of the man, unto whom God imputeth righteousness without works,* [then Psalm 32:1-2 is quoted] *saying, Blessed are they whose iniquities are forgiven, and whose sins are covered. Blessed is the man to whom the Lord will not impute sin.*

> Romans 4:6-8

David was prophesying and describing the day that you and I live in—when the Gospel is preached. It had been revealed unto David that a Savior was coming. Of course, he gave many prophecies concerning this and saw by the Spirit a wonderful day coming when we would be justified without the deeds of the law. Notice verse 8, how the Word says, "Blessed is the man to whom the Lord *will not* impute sin." It's not just "did not" or "does not," but *"will not."* God's Word

David knew that the real thing God was after was his heart.

plainly reveals that our past, present, and even future tense sin has been dealt with through the Lord Jesus Christ!

For additional study on this truth, I recommend my teachings entitled "Who You Are in the Spirit," "God's Attitude Toward Sin," "Identity in Christ" (which is the third message from *Harnessing Your Emotions*), and *The War Is Over*. They all dig into this aspect of Jesus dealing with our past, present, and even future tense sin in His atonement.

Paul was quoting David to show once again that the Old Testament had the Gospel preached in it. While repenting over his sin with Bathsheba (2 Sam. 11), David said:

> *Thou* [God] *desirest not sacrifice; else would I give it: thou delightest not in burnt offering. The sacrifices of God are a broken spirit: a broken and a contrite heart, O God, thou wilt not despise.*

> Psalm 51:16,17

What a radical statement for David's day. The law prescribed that certain sacrifices had to be offered for the sin that he had committed. However, according to the record of Scripture, he didn't offer those sacrifices. David simply repented before God with the knowledge that this was what the Lord was truly after. He had a revelation that all the Old Testament law was types and shadows of the Savior to come. David knew that the real thing God was after was his heart.

God loves us independent of our performance. Right standing with Him comes through faith.

Written for Us

In the next three verses of Romans 4, Paul returned to Abraham, saying:

> *Cometh this blessedness then upon the circumcision only, or upon the uncircumcision also? for we say that faith was reckoned to Abraham for righteousness. How*

was it then reckoned? when he was in circumcision, or in uncircumcision? Not in circumcision, but in uncircumcision. And he received the sign of circumcision, a seal of the righteousness of the faith which he had yet being uncircumcised.

Romans 4:9-11

Abraham was declared righteous thirteen years before he received the sign of this righteousness—circumcision. He was already righteous prior to being circumcised. This shows that it's not any of the things—even sacraments—that we do that make us righteous. It's not water baptism, the Lord's Supper, or our own personal holiness. Those things are by-products of our relationship with God. They're the fruit of right standing with Him, not the root of it.

In the latter part of Romans 4, Paul referred to Abraham once again as an example of believing God and his faith being counted unto him for righteousness. He concluded by saying that these things weren't just for Abraham alone, "But for us also, to whom it shall be imputed, if we believe on him that raised up Jesus our Lord from the dead; who was delivered for our offences, and was raised again for our justification" (Rom. 4:24-25).

In other words, Abraham's story was written for our sake. He did all these things that weren't right, but God still counted him righteous because of his faith. By this example, we can see that God loves us independent of our performance. Right standing with Him comes through faith.

Type and Shadow

> The only way to have peace with God is to be justified—made righteous—by faith, not by works or performance.

However, Abraham's sin (less than righteous performance) cost him. Lying two times to kings about his wife caused him hardship. (Gen. 12:11–18; 20:1–2.) Going into Hagar (Sarah's maid) and getting her pregnant caused him some grief. (Gen. 16:3–4.) Although his sins cost him, God didn't relate to Abraham based on his holiness (performance). If He had, Abraham would've been in serious trouble!

Abraham had married his half-sister. (Gen. 20:12.) According to the law, this was an abomination in God's sight, punishable by death. (Lev. 18:29.) If God had been dealing with Abraham according to his performance and giving him what he deserved, Abraham would have been killed. He wasn't perfect. But God wasn't dealing with him according to the law. Through Abraham's example, Paul showed how the Gospel was being preached in type and shadow even in the Old Testament.

Peace with God

Therefore being justified by faith, we have peace with God through our Lord Jesus Christ.

Romans 5:1

Paul was saying that the only way to have peace with God is to be justified—made righteous—by faith, not by works or performance.

I've dealt with literally thousands of people who have argued with me, saying, "You've got to be holy and do all these things to have God accept you." Without exception, those who believe and preach that do not have real peace in their lives. The only way that I have personally encountered real peace in my heart is through understanding these things. All of the people I've known who have experienced God's peace were those who had a revelation of justification by faith. That's the only way to ever have peace with God.

Otherwise, the burden of salvation is on your back. You have to constantly do this, do that, and hope that it's enough. There's never a time to just rest because you always have to perform. This is contrary to what Jesus Himself taught:

Come unto me, all ye that labour and are heavy laden, and I will give you rest. Take my yoke upon you, and learn of me; for I am meek and lowly in heart: and ye shall find rest unto your souls.

Matthew 11:28,29

Jesus was saying, "Come unto Me. You can't save yourself. You're trying to do something that's beyond your ability.

God's grace is consistent toward everyone, but not everyone reaps its benefits.

Come and let Me forgive you. Let Me heal you. Let Me deliver and prosper you based on grace and mercy—not your performance." Praise God—what a tremendous truth!

The only way we can have peace with God is through our Lord Jesus Christ.

Trust God—Let Go

We have peace with God.... By whom also we have access by faith into this grace wherein we stand, and rejoice in hope of the glory of God.

Romans 5:1,2

God's grace is consistent toward everyone, but not everyone reaps its benefits. Why? Because faith is how you gain access to God's grace.

Access means "admission."[1] If you go to the movies, you pay a price for admission. What's the price of admission to God's grace? Religion will tell you it's certain actions such as holiness—being good, attending church, paying your tithes. If you do this and that, then maybe God will give you access—admission.

This verse says that faith is what grants you admission, but faith in what? Not faith in yourself or your own performance, but faith in a Savior. Faith in God's grace—the Gospel of the

Lord Jesus Christ. That's the only thing you have to pay admission. That's the only thing that can grant you access into the grace of God. *Faith* is believing that the Gospel is true.

It's like the person dangling on a ledge five stories high. At this height, they could easily fall and be killed. However, the fire department has come to rescue them. Although they're a short distance away, they're ready to catch the dangling person. In order to be saved, the endangered individual needs to trust, let go, and fall into the arms of those waiting to rescue them below. Before they can be saved, they must let go.

Before we can receive salvation, we must quit trusting in ourselves. We must let go of our own goodness, which we've been maintaining, and put our trust in the Savior. It's a step of faith!

What We Deserve

This can be really scary because the entire world system reinforces our performance. To get along well with your parents as a child, you perform. You sing your ABCs, and they say, "Boy, you're wonderful because you do this." When you do well, you get a pat on the back. When you do a bad job, you get a pat on the rear. Your good performance is rewarded and your bad performance is punished.

> This knowledge of God's love in our hearts gives us boldness and confidence that we will not be put to shame.

In relationships—even in marriage—most people give us what we deserve. Your employer doesn't hire you by grace. They give you what you deserve. If you don't perform, you're fired. We've been trained that everything we get is what we deserve.

Therefore, letting go of our own performance and coming to God by faith can be pretty scary. Accepting salvation as a free gift—apart from any goodness on our own—is contrary to everything we've known. We just don't know how to relate—there's no role model for such grace. To enter in takes a real step of faith. It takes a genuine confidence in the Gospel so that we truly let go of our goodness and performance.

This is also the very reason why religious people fiercely oppose the Gospel. After working so hard to be holy and good, they hear someone like me saying that God accepts us based on faith, not based on our performance. This, in a sense, means that all of their good works and effort is wasted. That's not entirely true. Even though it doesn't gain us anything with God, it does benefit us personally in our relationships with people and by limiting Satan's access to us. But as far as earning us right standing with God, it's worthless. It doesn't provide us with enough goodness to be able to relate to Him. The only way we can relate to God is by grace and by putting faith in that grace. That's how we gain access.

What Love!

We have access by faith into this grace wherein we stand, and rejoice in hope of the glory of God. And not only so, but we glory in tribulations also: knowing that tribulation worketh patience; and patience, experience; and experience, hope: and hope maketh not ashamed; because the love of God is shed abroad in our hearts by the Holy Ghost which is given unto us.

Romans 5:2-5

Some people have used this scripture to teach things that aren't really what this passage is saying: "You need to embrace tribulation because your problems have been sent by God to help you." No, that's not what this is saying.

We're rejoicing in hope of the glory of God—not only in good times, but also in bad. How can we have such confidence? How can we rejoice when things are going bad? If God loved us enough that while we were still sinners He commended His love toward us, then how much more does He love us now that we're saints? This knowledge of God's love in our hearts gives us boldness and confidence that we will not be put to shame.

When we were yet without strength, in due time Christ died for the ungodly.

Romans 5:6

He died for the ungodly. Someone who isn't willing to admit they're ungodly cannot be saved. If they try to hold on to their goodness and performance, believing God owes it to them—maybe not 100 percent, but at least the 90 percent they "earned"—they cannot be saved.

Scarcely for a righteous man will one die: yet peradventure for a good man some would even dare to die. But God commendeth his love toward us, in that, while we were yet sinners, Christ died for us.

Romans 5:7,8

Can you imagine somebody dying for someone else? We can't even relate to that. Very seldom do you ever hear of someone dying for another. Somebody might die for a really good person, but Christ died for the ungodly. He valued us and died for us while we were yet sinners. What love!

CHAPTER 5

God's Free Gift

God commendeth his love toward us, in that, while we were yet sinners, Christ died for us.

Romans 5:8

Romans 5:8 is often taken out of context to make the point that God loves the sinner. That is a true statement. But in context, Paul was drawing a comparison. If you accept the fact that God loves the sinner, "Much more then, being now justified by his blood, we shall be saved from wrath through him" (Rom. 5:9).

This shows that when Paul was speaking of the Gospel being the power of God unto salvation, he was talking about more than just the initial born-again experience. In verses 8 and 9, he said that if God loved you and died for you when you

> You are not only saved by grace, but you also maintain your relationship with God by grace.

were ungodly, how much more does He love you now that you're born again.

The Drunkard

You are not only saved by grace, but you also maintain your relationship with God by grace. This means you are healed by grace, delivered by grace, and prospered by grace. None of the benefits of salvation come to you based on your performance. If you could understand that, then how much more would the love and faith of God abound in your life? Faith works by love (Gal. 5:6). If you understood how much God loves you, your faith would abound and you'd start seeing the benefits of your salvation manifest more.

> *If, when we were enemies, we were reconciled to God by the death of his Son, much more, being reconciled, we shall be saved by his life.*

Romans 5:10

Since religion has been preaching a performance-based relationship with God instead of preaching the Gospel, most people believe that the Lord loves them when they were a sinner, but He gets harder on them once they're saved. They may not use those exact words to express it, but let me give you an example to consider.

What would happen if someone came into your church service drunk? Most Christians would go up to them and start ministering God's love, mercy, and grace, saying, "Jesus loves you and died for your sin. He wants to forgive you and change your life." They would minister the Gospel to a total sinner—relationship with God based on His grace, not their performance.

What would happen if that person became born again and came back the next week drunk again? Those same people who ministered grace, forgiveness, and mercy, would turn around and say, "If you don't straighten up now that you're a saint, God is going to get you. Change your ways or the wrath of God will come upon you!"

> When it comes to our daily relationship with God, most people try to maintain it according to their performance.

Can you see how inconsistent that is? While they were a sinner, God would extend grace toward them. But after they're saved, they have to straighten up or face God's wrath. "Well, brother, you correct your own children harder than you correct somebody else's. Before you were His child, God may wink at certain things. But once you're born again, He's going to clamp down on you." That's not what God's Word teaches.

Maintained by Grace

As ye have therefore received Christ Jesus the Lord, so walk ye in him.

Colossians 2:6

The same way you were born again is the same way you should continue walking with Him. Sad to say, most people don't do that. Upon salvation, they sing, "Just as I am without one plea," and come to the Lord in the midst of sin—adultery, lying, stealing, all kinds of ungodliness. They receive the greatest gift ever—the initial born-again salvation experience. But then, after they're born again, they're in big trouble if they have the slightest little sin in their life. They think that God is liable to let them die of some disease just because they didn't do this or that. Let me ask you: How much did you read the Bible before you were born again? How much had you fasted and prayed before you were saved? How faithful were you in paying your tithes? The answer for nearly everyone is that you weren't faithful in any of these areas. You were just a rank sinner—"Just as I am." But see, you believed the Gospel!

"Salvation"—the initial born-again experience—has, by and large in evangelical Christianity, been preached by grace. But when it comes to our daily relationship with God, most people try to maintain it according to their performance. That's not the true Gospel. Remember, that's what Paul called a perversion of the Gospel. (Gal. 1:3–9.) It's not what Paul was preaching, nor the comparison he was making. According to Colossians 2:6, we should be maintaining our daily relationship with God in the same way as we were first born again.

This inconsistency—grace to be born again and works for daily maintenance—is the very reason why it's harder for many

Christians to receive healing than salvation. Technically speaking, it ought to be easier to receive healing after you're born again than it was to receive salvation when you were lost. If the devil had any right to stop you from receiving anything from God, he should have stopped you from being born again. You had no righteousness, no holiness whatsoever. But now that you're saved, your born-again spirit is always righteous and holy in God's sight. Even at your worst, you're better now than you ever were before you were born again. Yet, if you don't do everything just perfect, you're totally convinced that God won't answer your prayer because you don't deserve it.

> If you can accept that you were by nature a sinner, then you must also accept that now that you've been born again, you are by nature righteous.

Receiving healing isn't harder than receiving forgiveness. It's just that most Christians aren't trusting 100 percent in the grace of God for their healing the way they did for forgiveness of sins. Neither are they trusting 100 percent in the grace of God for His benefits like deliverance and prosperity. Instead, they're trusting in their own effort and hoping that Jesus will make up the difference. Wrong! This is falling for the devil's deception and putting our faith in our own performance. We must place our entire faith in the Gospel!

A Sinner by Nature

Wherefore, as by one man sin entered into the world, and death by sin; and so death passed upon all men, for that all have sinned.

Romans 5:12

Through Adam, we all became sinners. It wasn't our individual actions of sin that made us sinners, but this propensity for sin—this sin nature—that we inherited. We were born in sin. That's what makes us commit the individual actions of sin.

Most people recognize and can agree with being born with a sin nature—a sinner. My religious upbringing certainly ground that into me. However, in the latter part of Romans 5, Paul made another very important point. When you were saved, you were born again with a brand-new righteous nature. By placing your faith in the last Adam—the Lord Jesus Christ—you immediately received His holy nature. (1 Cor. 15:45.) If you can accept that you were by nature a sinner, then you must also accept that now that you've been born again, you are by nature righteous. You are no longer—by nature—a sinner. You've become righteous through what Jesus did for you.

Salvation isn't Jesus just forgiving you and pointing you in the right direction, saying, "Now I'm giving you another chance. Do it right from now on!" That's not what salvation is.

Salvation is coming to God, admitting that you've done it all wrong and that you can't save yourself, asking Him for His gift of salvation, and receiving it. And at the very moment you do, you become a brand-new person who is righteous in your born-again spirit (new nature).

Again, I'd like to encourage you to get hold of my teaching entitled *Spirit, Soul & Body.*[1] It's a more in-depth look at this than I am able to give here.

Born Again Righteous

You need to understand that when you were born again, your spirit instantly became righteous. It's not something you work at. It's not given to you based on your performance, but "It is the gift of God: not of works, lest any man should boast" (Eph. 2:8-9).

Notice that it is a gift, something you don't pay for or earn.

> *Not as the offence* [Adam's fall], *so also is the free gift. For if through the offence of one many be dead, much more the grace of God, and the gift by grace, which is by one man, Jesus Christ, hath abounded unto many.*
>
> Romans 5:15

Through Adam's fall, sin passed on to everybody. I didn't do anything to become a sinner. I was born into it. (Ps. 51:5.)

But when I was born again, I was born again into righteousness. I didn't do anything to earn it. I received it as a free gift.

> *Not as it was by one that sinned, so is the gift: for the judgment was by one to condemnation, but the free gift is of many offences unto justification.*

Romans 5:16

Adam's one sin produced many offenses throughout the human race. All of our actions of sin came out of the fact that we were by nature sinners. But having received the free gift of salvation—right standing with God—all of these offenses have been overcome as we've been brought to the place of being justified in the sight of God.

Accept the Truth

> *If by one man's offence death reigned by one; much more they which receive abundance of grace and of the gift of righteousness shall reign in life by one, Jesus Christ.*

Romans 5:17

It's a gift of righteousness that came through One—the Lord Jesus Christ. It doesn't come through what you do. Righteousness—right standing with God, being declared righteous in His sight—comes through faith. It's a gift from God.

The only thing you must do to access this grace is to have faith in what Jesus did for you.

> *Therefore as by the offence of one judgment came upon all men to condemnation; even so by the righteousness of one the free gift came upon all men unto justification of life.*
>
> Romans 5:18

That's the same point. Actually, five different times in these verses Paul made this same point. He repeated it over and over.

> *As by one man's disobedience many were made sinners, so by the obedience of one shall many be made righteous.*
>
> Romans 5:19

How can anyone get around this? If you accept the fact that you were born a sinner, then you must accept the truth that you are born again righteous. Righteousness isn't something you obtain through your effort. It's something you receive as a gift.

Holy Hippies?

These scriptures changed my life! Back in the late 1960s a friend of mine started telling me I was righteous and then suckered me into going to a Bible study he attended. This was during the time that I was still in a denominational church. I walked in the door of that Bible study and immediately became offended because a woman was leading. Women leaders didn't

> My head had the understanding, but my heart kept saying, "How can this be?"

square with my theology. Also, there were long-haired "hippies" in attendance. The denominational church I attended preached that long-haired hippies couldn't be saved. They taught that if a man's hair touched the collar of his shirt, he went straight to hell. So there I was in this Bible study with long-haired hippies and a woman leader. I was quite offended even before one word had been said.

Then the study began and they started talking about being righteous. I might have been able to tolerate them and not say anything as long as they'd just admit that they were sinners. But when these people started proclaiming that they were righteous, I couldn't handle it. I whipped out my three scriptures—"All have sinned, and come short of the glory of God" (Rom. 3:23), "There is none righteous, no, not one" (Rom. 3:10), "All our righteousnesses are as filthy rags" (Is. 64:6)—and just blasted them with both barrels.

To my surprise, instead of getting angry, they just continued to walk in love. For every one scripture I quoted about them being the scum of the earth, they quoted three or four about them being righteous. I didn't know there were scriptures like that. It just overwhelmed me! Although they didn't convince me, I determined when I left there that I would study this out for myself.

So I purchased a *Young's Analytical Concordance* and started studying every time the words *righteous* and *righteousness* were used in the Bible. After about a week of poring over the Word sixteen hours a day, I was intellectually convinced that I was righteous as a gift and not through what I did. I realized that these people were right in what they were saying.

But even though I could see it in my head, my heart had yet to embrace it. For so long I had related to the fact that I was by nature a sinner. So I struggled with this. My head had the understanding, but my heart kept saying, "How can this be?" These verses here in Romans 5 were what turned me around. They basically said that if I accepted the fact that I was born a sinner, then I also had to accept the truth that I had been born again righteous. It's not something I earn. It's not based on my performance. It's a gift—and I just had to accept it. If I believed that one side of the coin was true, then the other side had to be genuine too. Finally, I humbled myself and accepted it.

> Righteousness is knowing that you are accepted by your heavenly Father just as a child counts on their earthly father's acceptance.

These are powerful passages of scripture! If we truly understand what Paul was saying, there's no way we can still maintain that we must earn things from God based on our own holiness, righteousness, and works.

The week I studied these scriptures on righteousness culminated in an experience that the Lord used to drive home His point. I walked out on my back porch and sat down on the steps to meditate on what I'd seen in the Word. My dog, Honey, came running up to me the way she always did. At about five feet away, she stopped, rolled over on her side, and tentatively scooted the rest of the way. Even though I had never mistreated her, Honey's previous owners had beaten her with a chain as a puppy. Now she was a big German shepherd dog, but she always approached me like that. In frustration, I shouted, "Honey, just once I would like you to come up to me like a normal dog. Jump on me, sniff me, or anything else you like—but stop acting like I beat you!"

As soon as that left my lips, the Lord spoke in my heart and said, "That's the way I feel about you, Andrew. You always come before Me naming all of your sins, afraid that if you don't mention them, I will. Just once I'd like you to come to Me as a child approaches his father—confident of acceptance instead of fearful of rejection. Just jump up in My lap and say 'Abba, Father!'" (Rom. 8:15.)

That's what righteousness is. It's knowing that you are accepted by your heavenly Father just as a child counts on their earthly father's acceptance.

Grace Now Reigns

Moreover the law entered, that the offence might abound.

Romans 5:20

The law was given to show us that we are incapable of ever keeping it. It was given to make sin come alive in us and exercise such dominion over us that we would absolutely despair of ever trying to overcome sin on our own. It was given to bring us to the point of asking for righteousness as a gift. That's the purpose of the law.

Where sin abounded, grace did much more abound.

Romans 5:20

In other words, the law actually made us lust for things more, but God's grace was now revealed through properly understanding the real purpose of the law. It brought us to a place of understanding that it's only by the grace of God that we can ever overcome. Even though the law made us lust, it also showed us the grace of God—which was much greater than our sin.

As sin hath reigned unto death, even so might grace reign through righteousness unto eternal life by Jesus Christ our Lord.

Romans 5:21

The law was what made sin reign unto death. Empowered by the law, sin brought forth death. (Rom. 6:23.)

> Millions of people here in the United States have never heard the Gospel.

So sin dominated, ruled, and controlled us by the condemnation and guilt consciousness that came through the law. But now that we're in Christ and under the New Covenant, "grace reign[s] through righteousness unto eternal life by Jesus Christ our Lord" (Rom. 5:21).

Instead of law, grace is now the dominant factor. Grace is supposed to be ruling and controlling our lives. Sad to say, many people haven't heard that Gospel.

Saturated with Religion

I've heard people say, "Nobody in America should hear the Gospel twice until everyone else in the world has had an opportunity to hear it once!" I understand that the point they are trying to make is that it isn't fair for America to be saturated with Christian witness while millions of people around the world haven't even once heard the name of Jesus. I agree that international missions work is of the utmost priority. However, I disagree that America is saturated with the Gospel.

America has been saturated with religion. They've been loaded with condemnation and told, "You're going to hell if you don't repent!" Again, that's true, but it's not the Gospel. The Gospel—the message of God's grace, that He loves us independent of our performance and His goodness leads us to repentance—has not been properly proclaimed in America.

I am constantly ministering to people who don't understand God's grace. Although they've been to church their whole lives, they've never heard of it! They've heard ministers preach, "God is holy and just. You are unholy. If you don't repent, God is going to judge you. If you don't shape up, you're going to hell." Millions of people here in the United States have never heard the Gospel: "God loves you and is extending forgiveness for your sins. Everything that comes as a result of salvation—like forgiveness, righteousness, healing, deliverance, and prosperity—comes to you by grace through faith. It's not based on your performance, but God's grace. The only thing you must do to access this grace is to put faith in what God has done through Jesus Christ." The Gospel truly is the power of God unto salvation. (Rom. 1:16.) Sad to say, most people have never truly understood the Gospel.

> It's all about putting our faith in what Your Son did, and not what we do.

If you're having a problem in any area of your life today—forgiveness, healing, deliverance, prosperity—you're having a problem understanding the Gospel. As you understand God's grace, His love will abound in your life. Faith will work by love and everything you need will come through the power of the Gospel. The Gospel is the power of God!

What Does This Mean?

So what does this mean? Should we just go live in sin? Paul began dealing with this in Romans 6, which we'll be looking at next.

But first, I'd like to pray for you:

Father, please give my friend a revelation of the power of the Gospel today. Enable them to understand what salvation truly is and how You've provided for them everything they need as a free gift through Christ's death, burial, and resurrection. Please enlighten them to these truths from Your Word. As they begin to understand Your grace, thank You for setting them free from guilt, condemnation, and a performance mentality. It's all about putting our faith in what Your Son did, and not what we do. From this day forward, may Your grace be the foundation of my friend's daily relationship with You. Amen.

CHAPTER 6

Why Live Holy?

The Gospel is the power of God. It's good news—specifically, that our right standing with God is based on His grace, not our performance. The law was given to show us our need of a Savior. Salvation is more than just forgiveness of sins and the initial born-again experience. It includes everything purchased for us through the atonement of Jesus—like healing, deliverance, and prosperity.

The Question

In the first five chapters of Romans, Paul presented grace in such a strong and powerful way that it was inevitable for this question to arise:

> *What shall we say then? Shall we continue in sin, that grace may abound?*
>
> Romans 6:1

Romans is the definitive work on what grace really is.

Under the inspiration of the Holy Spirit, Paul had just expounded this subject of grace in masterful fashion. As I said before, Romans is the definitive work on what grace really is. Therefore, we could certainly say that Paul presented this truth in proper balance. However, three different times in Romans (3:8; 6:1; 6:15), Paul had to deal with this question: "What am I saying then? Am I saying that you can just go live in sin because God is dealing with you based on grace and not performance?"

Three times a man who presented this truth in perfect balance had to counter what he knew people were wondering in their hearts: *Let me see if I have this straight here, Paul. My sin isn't the issue. It's not separating me from God. My performance has no bearing on my right standing with Him. All I must do to access God's grace is place my faith in what Jesus Christ did. Are you saying that I can just go out and live in sin?* If Paul, presenting this properly, had to repeatedly deal with this question, how then can we think that we could present the Gospel any better so that no one would misunderstand it?

If we're truly preaching grace the way Paul did, it's inevitable that somebody will jump to this conclusion and ask, "Are you saying that I can just go live in sin?" Of course, Paul's answer to this in every instance was a resounding *no!* That's not what he was saying. That's not what I am saying. That's not what any true teacher of God's

Word is saying when they preach grace. But if the question doesn't come up, then we haven't communicated grace to the same extent Paul did.

In fact, if that question doesn't arise, then you haven't properly presented the Gospel. If you have emphasized God's grace sufficiently, then this should be a logical question that must be addressed.

God Forbid!

I understand that—by implication—this brings quite a bit of judgment upon what most people are calling "the Gospel" today.

The church I grew up in preached hellfire and damnation, emphasizing over and over again the fact that we were born sinners. They focused on the judgment end of it but didn't present the good news. God's grace and our new nature were never emphasized. While listening to such "Gospel," I didn't wonder even once, *Can I just go live in sin?* The way the Bible was presented, I was continually made aware of sin. They told me I sinned every day—constantly—and needed to confess it, even if I wasn't aware of a specific action. I was under so

If our holiness isn't what gains us favor with God, then why bother?

much condemnation and sin-consciousness that I never mistook what was being preached to me as saying that I could just go live in sin if I wanted. Although the people ministering in the denomination I grew up in would probably take this as a tremendous compliment, that's certainly not the same Gospel Paul preached.

Paul presented the Gospel—the grace of God—in such a way that he was misunderstood. If we're presenting the Gospel properly today, then we're going to have to come back and answer this question: "Are you saying then that I can just go live in sin?" If you don't have to deal with this thought in the minds of your hearers, then you haven't yet presented the Gospel in the same way as Paul.

That being said, let me add that Paul was not encouraging sin. In Romans 6:2, he began to answer this question saying, "God forbid." This was the strongest renunciation Paul could have made in the Greek language without employing some type of profanity. This was an emphatic, absolute denial. He was saying, "No! Absolutely not! Let it never be!"

Why then wasn't Paul's attitude, "Hey, since it's by God's grace, just keep living in sin"? If our sin isn't what's stopping God from moving in our lives, and it's not our holiness that earns His blessing, but it's His grace only; then what is the purpose of holiness? Why live holy? If our holiness isn't what gains us favor with God, then why bother?

The Purpose of Holiness

Of course, most people today are well versed in the fact that the Bible teaches us to live holy. I'm not going to take time to go into all that. But I do want to look at what Paul said here in Romans 6 about why we should live holy. What is the purpose of holiness?

Paul gave two reasons for, "Why live holy?" The first begins here in verse 2.

> *How shall we, that are dead to sin, live any longer therein?*
>
> Romans 6:2

The number one reason why a Christian doesn't live in sin is because we are no longer by nature a child of the devil. After being born again, it's not our nature to sin anymore. I recognize this raises several questions, which we'll come back and consider. But before we do, let's look at where he raised the question again and supplied us with reason number two.

> Anyone who preaches the grace of God correctly is not advocating living in sin.

> *What then? shall we sin, because we are not under the law, but under grace? God forbid. Know ye not, that to whom ye yield yourselves servants to obey, his servants ye are to whom ye obey; whether of sin unto death, or of obedience unto righteousness?*
>
> Romans 6:15,16

The second reason to live holy is: Living holy will stop Satan's inroads into your life. If you are living in sin, you're yielding yourself to the author of sin. This allows the devil to bring death and destruction into your life. If you yield yourself to holiness, then you're yielding yourself to God who is the author of that holiness. This produces godly results.

In summary, the two reasons for a Christian to live holy are:

> Meeting with other believers is important because it changes your heart toward God—not His toward you.

It's our nature to live holy, and

Living holy stops Satan's inroads into our lives.

Paul was certainly not advocating sin. I'm not advocating sin. Anyone who preaches the grace of God correctly is not advocating living in sin. We're just saying that our motive for living holy is not to get God to accept us. We live holy because it's our nature to live that way, and we don't want to give the devil any access into our lives.

Holiness Helps You

For a born-again believer, living holy is a fruit—not a root—of salvation. It's a by-product of living in right relationship with

God, but not a means to obtain it. Now that's a powerful reve-lation you need to get hold of!

Of course a Christian is supposed to be holy. Holiness is important, probably more important than you've ever heard preached. But why? Why is it so important?

Most people who don't understand grace operate under a legalistic mindset and relate to God based on their performance. These kinds of people say that the reason why holiness is so important is that it's how God moves in your life: "He moves directly proportional to your holiness." That's not true. That's not what this scripture is teaching.

Many people believe that the reason why they are supposed to attend church is that God is somehow keeping track of their attendance. If you attend well, then you may get your prayers answered. If you don't attend, then God will be upset with you and probably won't answer your prayers or move on your behalf. That's not true.

God doesn't move in your life based on your church atten-dance. If you never went to church again, God would love you exactly the same. But you wouldn't love God exactly the same. You'd miss out on fellowshipping with other believers and the encouragement and challenge it brings. You wouldn't hear and apply the Word of God in the same way while sitting at home all by yourself. Meeting with other believers is important because it changes your heart toward God—not His toward you.

If you never went to church again, God would love you just the same. But you'd be foolish not to attend church because you wouldn't love Him the same. Can you see how holiness (attending church) helps you?

It's your nature to live that way (worship, fellowship, and study God's Word with other believers), and

It helps you resist the devil (by being around other Christians and in the Word together).

Run to Win

If you never studied the Word again, God would love you exactly the same. But you wouldn't love God the same because you wouldn't have the revelation of His truth. You'd be thinking according to someone's opinion. You aren't really free to just develop your own opinions about God. Somebody is going to influence you, one way or another. Either you'll be influenced by the death, negativism, and wrong conceptions of the world and religion, or you'll get into God's Word and learn "the truth, and the truth shall make you free" (John 8:32).

> *Sanctify them* [or make them holy] *through thy truth: thy word is truth.*
>
> John 17:17

Remember, being in God's Word changes your heart toward Him. It softens your heart, but God loves you just the same if you never study His Word.

> Lay the weights aside and be more effective. Run to win!

Since God's love toward us doesn't change based on our performance, does this mean we shouldn't get into the Word? No! If we're truly born again, it's our nature to hunger for the truth—and as we just saw, the Word is the source of truth. If we're aware of the reality that we are in a battle and Satan is coming against us, then we'll realize that it's to our advantage to get into the Word because it changes our heart and corrects our attitudes. Being in God's Word gives us revelation and helps keep the devil from having access into our lives.

I'm advocating the same standards as those who demand holiness, but from an entirely different motive. Go to church, pay your tithes, study the Word, love people, get rid of bitterness and anger—keep all the standards. I'm advocating holiness, but for totally different reasons. This is the point Paul was making. The motive for holiness changed!

You shouldn't be living holy and thinking, *If I'm holy enough, God will love me... accept me... answer my prayers... heal me... prosper me....* All of these things—your entire relationship with God—must be based on grace. If you're truly born again, you desire to live holy and to minimize Satan's opportunities against you.

Let us lay aside every weight, and the sin which doth so easily beset us, and let us run with patience the race that is set before us.

Hebrews 12:1

You're a runner running the race of life. The person who's organized the race and put it on may not be mad at you if you don't finish first, but if you have weights—sins—holding you back, it's definitely going to hinder you in running for the Lord. You won't be as effective as someone else. God won't love you less, but you might love Him less. Lay the weights aside and be more effective. Run to win!

Wrong motivation gets wrong results.

Motive Is Everything

Some may say, "Well, living holy is still the bottom line. What's the big deal?"

Motive is everything! According to God's Word, your motive is actually more important than your action.

Though I bestow all my goods to feed the poor, and though I give my body to be burned, and have not charity [God's kind of love], *it profiteth me nothing.*

1 Corinthians 13:3

Holy acts—in this case giving to the poor or even laying down your life for another—profit you nothing unless they're done motivated by God's kind of love. If your motivation for living holy—giving finances, or sacrificing your life for someone else, for example—is debt, obligation, or trying to earn something, then your motive is wrong. You aren't doing it out of a love response for what the Lord has done, but you're doing it to try to gain a positive response from God. You believe that God is responding to you, instead of you responding to Him. If that's your motive, it profits you nothing!

This is exactly why so many people aren't healed, delivered, and prospered. They're doing the right things—studying the Word, paying their tithes, among others—but they are putting their faith in what they are doing. They're thinking, *God, is it enough? Now will You move in my life?* Wrong motivation gets wrong results. That's not true Bible faith. True Bible faith must be in what God has done for us, not in what we are doing for God!

CHAPTER 7

Dead to Sin

Let's return to Romans 6:2 and go into some detail concerning this first reason Paul gave for "Why live holy?"

How shall we, who are dead to sin, live any longer therein?

We need to understand what truly happened the moment we were born again. The old sin nature that we were born with was crucified, dead, and buried; and we were born again with a brand-new righteous nature. The old nature that expressed itself through sin is now gone. A new nature, which desires to express itself through holy living, has now taken its place.

For further study, I highly recommend my teaching on *Spirit, Soul & Body.*[1] In it, I expound much more upon these foundational truths concerning what happened inside you the instant you were born again. Understanding the interaction between your body, soul, and born-again spirit will set you free to confidently walk in intimacy with the Lord and actually experience the abundant life He's provided.

Buried with Him

Know ye not, that so many of us as were baptized into
Jesus Christ were baptized into his death?

Romans 6:3

This isn't talking about water baptism. Some people teach that, but Scripture plainly reveals that there is more than one baptism. In Hebrews 6:2, the Word talks about "the doctrine of baptisms [plural]." First Corinthians 12:13 describes us being baptized by the Spirit into the body of Christ, which is what Romans 6:3 is talking about.

Other baptisms, besides this one, include the baptism in the Holy Spirit and water baptism. (See Acts 11:16.) As you can see, there are several New Testament baptisms. Therefore, it's important to recognize which one a given passage of scripture is referring to. Is it talking about the Holy Spirit baptizing someone just born again into the body of Christ, an older Christian baptizing a new convert in water, or Jesus baptizing a believer with the Holy Spirit and fire?

In Romans 6:3, this passage of scripture is referring to how the Holy Spirit supernaturally places us into the body of Christ the instant we're born again. When that happened, we were baptized into His death. This means we partook of Jesus' death.

Therefore we are buried with [Jesus] *by baptism into*
death: that like as Christ was raised up from the dead by the

glory of the Father, even so we also should walk in newness
of life. For if we have been [past tense] *planted together in*
the likeness of his death, we shall be also in the likeness of
his resurrection: knowing this.

Romans 6:4-6

We participated in Jesus' death when the Holy Spirit placed
us in Christ and made the things that He died to accomplish a
reality in our life. That happened in the past, the instant we were
born again. But since appropriating what Jesus did for us takes
our cooperation, the scripture then refers to the end result. In
other words, every Christian has participated in the death of
their old man through Jesus. But we haven't all participated yet
in His resurrection life, which is a by-product of being placed
in His body, because we must know this:

Our old man is crucified with him, that the body of sin
might be destroyed, that henceforth we should not serve sin.

Romans 6:6

Action or Nature?

We are now dead to sin. It's important to understand that
Paul was talking about sin (sin nature), not sins (individual
actions of sin). Out of the forty-nine times this word *sin* is used
in Romans (sin, thirty-seven times; sins, four times; sinned, five

> You can't change your nature simply by decreasing your actions of sin!

times; sinners, two times; sinner, one time), forty-seven times it's talking about the old sin nature ("old self" in the NIV), not individual actions of sin. We know this because the Greek word from which *sin* and *sins* was translated forty-seven out of the forty-nine times isn't a verb, but a noun.[2] If you remember English class, a noun always describes a person, place, or thing.

Only two times in the entire book of Romans is *sin* referred to as an action:

> *Whom God hath set forth to be a propitiation through faith in his blood, to declare his righteousness for the remission of sins* [actions of sin] *that are past, through the forbearance of God.*
>
> Romans 3:25

> *What then? shall we sin* [commit actions of sin], *because we are not under the law, but under grace? God forbid.*
>
> Romans 6:15

But in the rest of Romans, the word *sin* and all its other English forms (sins, sinned, sinners, sinner) were translated from a Greek noun.[3] Therefore, in the entire book of Romans, other than the verses in 3:25 and 6:15, Paul was referring to the driving force that compelled us to sin (our old sin nature), not individual acts of sin.

Children of Wrath

Wherefore, as by one man sin entered into the world, and death by sin; and so death passed upon all men, for that all have sinned.

Romans 5:12

Through Adam, sin entered into the world—not actions of sin, but the sin nature. You were born a child of the devil.

*We all... were **by nature** the children of wrath, even as others.*

Ephesians 2:3

Ye [non-believers] *are of your father the devil, and the lusts of your father ye will do.*

John 8:44

What makes people commit actions of sin is the fact that they have a sin nature. Even if somehow or other we could deal with our actions of sin and restrain the amount of sin we commit (like the religious nonbelievers Jesus was speaking to in John 8:44), there's still no human way to deal with that sin nature. You can't change your nature simply by decreasing your actions of sin! This is what most legalistic people focus on. They wrongly emphasize actions and holiness as

Through Jesus Christ, God went to the very root of sin—our sin nature—and dealt with it.

the basis of their relationship with God. "Don't lust or steal. Don't commit adultery. Don't do these things. If you can just act right, then you'll be right." That's exactly opposite of what the Word teaches. The reason nonbelievers act wrong is because they have a wrong nature driving and compelling them to do actions of sin.

"Knowing This"

Through Jesus Christ, God went to the very root of sin—our sin nature—and dealt with it. He didn't just give us the ability to overcome actions of sin, but He dealt with the part of us that was corrupted and forcing us to live in sin. When Jesus died on the cross, He didn't take only our physical actions of sin, but He also took the very root of sin—our sin nature—upon Himself.

> *He hath made him to be sin for us, who knew no sin; that we might be made the righteousness of God in him.*
>
> 2 Corinthians 5:21

Jesus didn't just bear sin—He became sin. He took that sin nature upon Himself and suffered that separation from God. He endured our rejection and punishment from God for sin and died to that old sin nature. Jesus literally and completely put it to death and was resurrected from the dead with a brand-new life, which is no longer corrupted or susceptible to sin. This brand-new life doesn't have that propensity, drive, or constant motivation for sin in it. Because of that, the actions of sin have no more dominion or place in His life.

> *If we have been planted together in the likeness of his death, we shall be also in the likeness of his resurrection: knowing this.*
>
> Romans 6:5,6

Through Christ, we also are dead with Him unto sin *and* we will also be in the likeness of His resurrection *when we know this:*

> *Our old man* [our old sin nature] *is crucified with him, that the body of sin might be destroyed, that henceforth we should not serve sin. For he that is dead is freed from sin.*
>
> Romans 6:6,7

Until your mind is renewed, you'll continue functioning the way you were previously programmed.

In other words, one of the reasons why people who have truly been born again still live in sin is because they don't know what has happened to them. They don't know that their old sin nature has been crucified and put to death in Christ. You have to know this!

Prior Programming

In our born-again spirit, we've been set free. In our recreated righteous spirit, we no longer have the nature of the devil driving us to be like him anymore. However, your spirit isn't the only thing influencing your heart. You also have an unrenewed mind that has been taught and trained how to act in a certain way—in accordance with your old sin nature. Before being born again, your old nature—reinforced by everything in this world system—taught you how to think selfishly, how to operate in anger, bitterness, fear, unbelief, and in a number of other fleshly ways. Until your mind is renewed, you'll continue functioning the way you were previously programmed.

Your natural mind is similar to a computer. It can do only what it's been programmed to do. Once you're in Christ, you have been freed from sin. That old man has been put to death and there's no longer a sin nature compelling you to live in sin. But you might still be living in sin if you haven't reprogrammed yourself by renewing your mind. As a matter of fact, many Christians still seem driven to sin.

By observation, many people can't see any real difference in their motivation for sin before and after they're born again. Although it seems like we still have this drive toward sin, these scriptures tell us that it's not our old self, our old sin nature, our old man compelling us to sin, but rather an unrenewed mind. That old man taught us to act certain ways.

Once you know this—that your old man is crucified and dead—then the body of sin (the programming in your unrenewed mind that it left behind) can be destroyed so that henceforth you should not serve sin. If you know these things, then you can break this dominion of sin in your life. Sadly, most Christians are still laboring under this false impression that there's still a part of them sold out to the devil and there's nothing they can do about it.

You may be wondering, *Well, what about Romans 7?* Later in this book, I'll be contrasting Romans 7 and 8 in detail. But I don't believe the Scripture teaches that born-again believers still have this old man. This is exactly what Paul was talking about here in the first half of Romans 6. Your old man was crucified with Christ. You're dead. "But if I'm dead, then why am I still committing sin and still experiencing this drive toward sin in certain areas? If I'm dead, wouldn't that be different?" Not unless you've renewed your mind.

Your natural mind is going to function the way it was programmed until it's reprogrammed. You can have the life of God in your born-again spirit and be a totally brand-new being in your spirit, but you can still experience a bent toward certain sins. Your mind is just following its prior programming.

Wall-to-Wall Holy Ghost

I don't remember buttoning my shirt this morning because this action has become almost automatic to me. Since I'm not even conscious anymore of the fact that I did it, it's become "natural" for me. But it hasn't always been that way. I remember struggling to button my shirt as a kid. It always seemed to come out wrong. Although learning to button my shirt took me some effort, I've learned it so well that now it's just like it's my nature.

I remember sitting on a couch in our home and my grand-mother teaching me to tie my shoes. It was an ordeal then, but now I don't even think about it. It's automatic. It's natural. I just tie my shoes when I need to without any conscious effort.

That's the same way it is with our habits, lusts, desires, and drive for sin. Before we were born again, we had a nature that just drove us toward sin. Our actions of sin came because of our nature of sin. This nature drove us and was reinforced through society. Everybody else had an old nature too, so we were bombarded from every angle all the time with how to be selfish, self-centered, hate people, advance ourselves, and take advantage of others. We've been taught how to be depressed, constantly look on the negative side of things, be mean to others, and many other sinful actions. All of these things are acquired traits from the nature that was originally on the inside of us driving us to do them. But now that we're in Christ, it's not that way anymore. That old nature isn't there driving us anymore.

The only thing causing us to remain under this bondage of sin is an unrenewed mind. We don't know that we've been freed. We think, *I'm only human. I'm just a man,* or *I'm just a woman,* and sing songs like, "One Day at a Time, Sweet Jesus." But it's not true. We're not only human. We're not just a man, or just a woman. We've been born again and there's now a brand-new born-again part of us. One-third of us is wall-to-wall Holy Ghost. We're a new person in Christ. We have a new nature in Him.

If I don't know and understand this, if I think that I'm only human, then when supernatural opposition comes, when demonic powers arise against me, and when temptations get strong, I might resist for a while, but then I'll think, *Well, I'm only human. I'm just a man. I can only do so much. There are limits to what I can stand,* and then I'll wind up giving in to the temptation.

> All born-again believers in Jesus Christ have been freed from the dominion of their old sin nature.

I need to understand that I'm a new person in Christ with a brand-new nature full of God's supernatural ability on the inside of me. If I know this and I'm grounded in it so much that what I see, taste, hear, smell, and feel doesn't dominate me, then my opinion of my born-again self is based on God's Word. If that's controlling and dominating me, then I can overcome those temptations and lusts for sin.

F-R-E-E-D *from Sin*

Back in the 1800s, President Abraham Lincoln issued the Emancipation Proclamation that freed all of the slaves in the

USA. They were freed—F-R-E-E-D—but they weren't neces-
sarily free—F-R-E-E. There are documented cases of a number
of African Americans who did not hear about the Emancipation
Proclamation. Some of the slave owners didn't inform their
slaves. Back in those days, they didn't have access to mass
media and communications the way we do today. It took some
of those slaves years to hear through the grapevine that they had
been freed.

They were freed, but they weren't free because they didn't
know something. They could have been free, but it was
dependent upon them knowing the truth, and then having
enough boldness to step out and test that truth by standing up
against that old master and drawing on the legal system's power
and authority to back them up.

> *He that is dead is freed from sin.*
>
> Romans 6:7

All born-again believers in Jesus Christ have been freed
from the dominion of their old sin nature. Does that mean that
we're going to walk free? Well, that depends on how much
we know.

CHAPTER 8

Renew Your Mind

A friend of mine in a church once heard me teach on born-again believers being dead to sin. He didn't say anything to me while I was ministering, but I listened to the tapes later and heard his comments. After I left, he had stood up and ridiculed this truth, saying, "I don't understand what Andrew was trying to say, but anybody can tell by observation that we still have this tendency toward sin. Although I hate to disagree with him, he's totally wrong in this area. We still have a tendency toward sin!"

I'm not saying that we don't have a tendency, but I am saying that the tendency now is not a nature that compels us toward sin. It's just an unrenewed mind—and that mind is a very compelling force.

Virtual Reality

When you go over that first high peak on a roller-coaster and start coming down the hill at breakneck speed, you physically feel as if your stomach is coming up into your throat. Do you remember that feeling? It was based on fact—actually riding the roller-coaster. It's something that really happened. But your mind was also involved. Therefore, by using a virtual reality system on your eyes and ears, you can fool your mind into thinking you're back on that roller-coaster again. Then, as you "go down that first hill," you can physically experience the feeling of your stomach coming up into your throat feeling again—even though it's not really happening. You can experience those same physical sensations and feelings as before by nothing more than inducing it through the mind.

You can do the same thing with someone who has a problem going round and round and round without feeling sick and throwing up. They could be sitting absolutely still with a virtual reality system on. However, because that system is feeding their mind images of going round and round and round, you can induce that same feeling—even to the point of that person throwing up—with nothing physical actually happening. No longer are there physical things driving it. It's all in the mind. The mind has been taught how to react to sight and sound. The mind can induce many of these same responses that were once induced by actual physical reality.

The old man used to drive our thinking. Because of that, we experienced lust and desire for sin. It was true that there was something inside each of us—a nature—that drove us toward sin. But that nature died the moment we became born again. If you are born again, you're no longer being driven toward sin by some part of you that is—by nature—a child of the devil. All that's happening now is that something's playing with your mind. Satan plays on these old thought patterns that we had toward sin. It's our unrenewed mind that drives us to sin. In order to break this, we must recognize that *Hey, this isn't really happening!*

If you knew that you had a virtual reality system on and understood that you were really just sitting in a chair, you could actually keep your mind (and body) from "experiencing" the same degree of feeling and motion. If you knew that it was these things on your head covering your eyes and ears that were the true source of these thoughts—and not reality—you could control your reactions and response to it. By acting on that knowledge—*This isn't really happening, but is just being imposed upon me*—you could calm yourself down, lessen the sick feeling, and keep yourself from throwing up.

You can do the same thing spiritually, by saying, "I don't care what things look like. I know I'm dead to that old sin nature that drove me at one time. That thing died with Christ and now it's gone. I have a brand-new righteous nature on the inside of me and I refuse to submit any longer to this old

> The key to the
> Christian life is
> the renewing of
> the mind.

programming." You might experience some of the same emotions that you had before you were born again, but the truth is that you are dead to that sin. You are no longer being driven to live it. It's just an unrenewed mind that keeps these thoughts coming. And as long as your mind remains unrenewed, you'll continue operating the way you did before under the same impulses, situations, and temptations. But as you renew your mind, you'll be able to overcome them. The key is renewing your mind!

Transformed by Renewal

I beseech you therefore, brethren, by the mercies of God, that ye present your bodies a living sacrifice, holy, acceptable unto God, which is your reasonable service. And be not conformed to this world: but be ye transformed by the renewing of your mind, that ye may prove what is that good, and acceptable, and perfect, will of God.

Romans 12:1,2

The word "transformed" here is the Greek word *metamorphoo*.[1] It's the word from which we get "metamorphosis." A little caterpillar spins a cocoon and then comes out a butterfly. If you want this kind of change in your life, the way it happens is by the renewing of your mind.

The key to the Christian life is the renewing of the mind. When you were born again, your spirit changed—but your natural mind didn't. It remained unrenewed. You don't need more of God in your heart. You already have all of God there. Everything you need is already in your born-again spirit—the life of God, the faith of God, the joy of God, the peace of God, the anointing of God, and everything else that's of God—but it's only going to manifest itself in your life to the degree you renew your mind.

If you still think that you're just an old sinner saved by grace and it's just a matter of time before that sin nature drives you to do something, you're believing something contrary to Scripture. Stop embracing this wrong idea and confessing, "I'm just a sinner saved by grace." Acknowledge instead the truth that your old nature's hold on you has been broken. You are now dead with Christ to sin. All you're dealing with now is what Romans 6:6 calls, "the body of sin." It's not the actual sin nature itself, but the body it left behind.

Twitching Corpses

Physical death is when your spirit separates from your body.

> *As the body without the spirit is dead, so faith without works is dead also.*

> James 2:26

We don't have
to live unto
sin anymore.

When someone's spirit leaves their body, that's death. Although that spirit goes to be with the Lord, it leaves behind a body. For a brief period of time, that body doesn't decay, but still looks like the person who once lived in it. As a matter of fact, a dead body can still have some reactions. For instance, if you cut a snake's head off, the body will slither around and appear alive. If you chop off a chicken's head, it'll flop around too. Even though it's dead, the body can still react.

A friend of mine worked in the morgue on the thirteenth floor of Parkland Hospital in Dallas, Texas. One time he pulled out a dead man on a slab and then turned around to get something. When he looked back, this body had sat up with its eyes and mouth wide open. He was just sitting there with his arms dangling at his side. My friend nearly jumped out the window! He thought this guy was alive and it scared him.

My friend ran and got somebody. They came back in, checked this fellow out, and pushed the body back down. Even though this guy was dead, electrical types of reactions were causing his body to twitch and move. He was totally dead, but his body was still reacting.

Our old man is dead, but he left behind a "body." I'm not talking about our physical flesh and bones body. I mean the programming in the mind—the attitudes and wrong thinking. That's "the body of sin" that Paul was talking about, and we need to know this: "Our old man is crucified with [Jesus]" (Rom. 6:6).

Then, the next step is to destroy that body of sin. We do that by systematically tearing down those wrong thoughts and emotions with the Word of God and replacing them with godly thoughts and emotions. The end result of this process called *renewing the mind* is "that henceforth we should not serve sin" (v. 6).

The good news is that Jesus went to the very root of the sin problem. He dealt decisively with that sin nature, and—in Christ—we also have died to sin. Therefore, we don't have to live unto sin anymore. If we just knew and understood this, it would change our life!

Alive unto God

Now if we be dead with Christ, we believe that we shall also live with him.

Romans 6:8

We are dead with Christ, but living with Him is dependent upon what we know.

Knowing that Christ being raised from the dead dieth no more; death hath no more dominion over him.

Romans 6:9

> We need to arm ourselves by getting the same mind that Jesus now has toward sin.

It's "knowing" again. As these two verses say, "We believe that we shall also live with him: *knowing* that…." If you don't know this, if you aren't really established in it, then you won't experience that resurrection life, victory, and power that belongs to us. You have to know "that Christ being raised from the dead dieth no more; death hath no more dominion over him" (v. 9).

Most people understand that Jesus isn't struggling with sin. He's not up there denying Himself and trying to put down His old sin nature. With Christ, that's over with. Jesus is now completely holy and totally pure.

> *In that he died, he died unto sin once: but in that he liveth, he liveth unto God.*
>
> Romans 6:10

Again, that's talking about Jesus. Most people would agree with that. But look at what the next verse says:

> *Likewise* [in the same manner] *reckon ye also yourselves to be dead indeed unto sin, but alive unto God through Jesus Christ our Lord.*
>
> Romans 6:11

What a strong statement! You need to see yourself dead to sin the same way that Christ is dead to sin. Do you think that

Jesus still has an old sin nature plus a new righteous nature on the inside of Him, and He's struggling between the two? Of course not! Jesus is dead to sin. He's no longer dealing with any propensity, sin nature, or actual sin drive. He took that into His own body and suffered for it. It's dead, buried, and gone. We need to see ourselves just like Jesus—resurrected unto new life in God.

Let Not Sin Reign

Arm yourselves likewise with the same mind: for he that hath suffered in the flesh hath ceased from sin.

1 Peter 4:1

Some people teach that this means, "The more you suffer, the more it'll break the dominion of sin in your life." That's certainly not true. Some of the people who have suffered the most are some of the greatest sinners. This really means that Jesus—the One who suffered in the flesh by taking our sins into His own body on the cross and died for us—has ceased from sin. Sin has no more dominion over Him.

We need to arm ourselves by getting the same mind that Jesus now has toward sin. He's not relating to sin. He doesn't feel like a part of Himself is bound by nature to sin. He certainly knows better than that!

So both 1 Peter 4:1 and Romans 6:11 tell us we need to have this same attitude as Christ toward sin. Here's the result of this attitude:

> *Let not sin therefore reign in your mortal body, that ye should obey it in the lusts thereof.*

> Romans 6:12

"Let not." This means that you do have the power to stop sin—the noun *sin*—from reigning in your life. The sin nature itself is dead and gone, but it's up to you whether you let it continue to reign through the body—prior programming—it left behind. Don't let the tendency you have toward sin because of an unrenewed mind reign in your mortal body. Since the Word commands you not to do this, this shows that you do have the power to deny sin the right to reign in your life.

"Not Under the Law..."

> *Neither yield ye your members as instruments of unright-eousness unto sin: but yield yourselves unto God, as those that are alive from the dead, and your members as instruments of righteousness unto God. For sin shall not have dominion over you: for ye are not under the law, but under grace.*

> Romans 6:13,14

The law was not given to break the dominion of sin, but to give sin dominion over us. The law strengthened sin. (1 Cor.

15:56.) The law made sin revive and come alive. (Rom. 7:9.) The law actually empowered sin because sin was already present in the sin nature. People were deceived, thinking, *If I'll just quit living in the actions of sin, then I'll be okay.* Even if they could do that (which they couldn't) and limited the number of sin actions they committed and somehow or another felt good about themselves, they still couldn't change their sin nature. It was still there. It

> God did not strap Adam and Eve with a bunch of rules and regulations. He gave them freedom.

might be a little bit dormant. It might be soothed over by all of these good works being done, but the truth is that we can't change our nature just by acting good.

So the Lord had to bring us out of this deception. How did He do it? He started saying, "Thou shalt not..." Then, when we heard a commandment not to do something, we lusted for the very thing we were forbidden to do.

As a kid, how did you get somebody to do something they didn't want to do? You'd just say real sarcastically, "You can't do it. What are you, chicken? You sissy! I bet you can't do it." The moment you told someone they couldn't do it, they'd break their neck trying.

Back in my running days, I was competing in a 6.2 mile race. When I was about a quarter of a mile from the finish line, this other runner started to pass me. I tried to keep up with him, but I was out of juice. I had turned in a personal record and just didn't have anything left. This guy could tell I tried to keep up with him. He looked back over his shoulder and said very sarcastically, "You can do better than that!" Once he said that, it's like I turned into the Incredible Hulk. My afterburners kicked in and I beat him in the last quarter mile of that race by 100 yards! I don't know where that strength came from, but there's just something about someone telling us we can't do something that makes us want to do it.

> We didn't produce our sin nature and we certainly can't produce our new nature.

Most of us have probably experienced something similar to that. There's just something inside us that goes off when we hear, "Thou shalt not..." and causes us to respond, "Bless God, I shall!" Something inside us just reacts because God didn't create us to be dominated by rules and regulations.

God did not strap Adam and Eve with a bunch of rules and regulations. He gave them freedom. When the law came, its purpose wasn't to break sin's dominion over your life. Rather, it was to illustrate, "Hey, you're hopelessly bound to this sin nature. You can't change yourself just by improving a bit. You need help! And to prove it to you, I'm going to show you what's in your heart. Thou shalt not commit adultery." All of a sudden, sin revived and you began to lust for everything God told you not to do.

While listening to me teach on this subject, a man decided to check this out for himself. In his backyard, his son and some friends had been playing well for over half an hour. So he walked up and told them, "Hey kids, you're doing great. But whatever you do, thou shalt not spit on this flower!" Then he went back into his house and looked out the window. Half the kids went right over and spit on that flower. The others just stood there with their mouths open and drooling—wishing they had enough nerve to spit on the flower. They immediately lusted for the thing they were commanded not to have.

"...But Under Grace"

That's what the law did. It actually gave sin—this sin nature—dominion over us. It made sin—the noun *sin*—come alive and begin to lust for everything we were told we couldn't have. The purpose was to bring us out of our deception and recognize that even though we might have overcome individual acts of sin, that sin nature was still there. We were by nature children of the devil and the only way out of it was to receive a brand-new nature. And that's something we can't produce. We didn't produce our sin nature and we certainly can't produce our new nature. We must receive it as a gift from God.

Grace now reigns!

So in Romans 6:14, Paul said that this old sin nature "shall not have dominion over you: for ye are not under the law, but under grace."

CHAPTER 9

Whose Servant Are You?

As sin hath reigned unto death, even so might grace reign through righteousness unto eternal life by Jesus Christ our Lord.

Romans 5:21

Sin once reigned unto death, but now grace reigns unto eternal life. Grace now reigns! When you begin to understand the grace of God, it allows eternal life to function in you the same way that the Old Testament law made lust revive and come through you.

Yielded to Satan or Jesus?

What then? shall we sin [commit sinful actions], *because we are not under the law, but under grace? God forbid.*

Romans 6:15

Then Paul went into the second reason for living holy:

> *Know ye not, that to whom ye yield yourselves servants*
> *to obey, his servants ye are to whom ye obey; whether of sin*
> *unto death, or of obedience unto righteousness?*
>
> Romans 6:16

If you live an unholy life, you're giving Satan access to you.

> *The thief cometh not, but for to steal, and to kill, and to*
> *destroy: I* [Jesus] *am come that they might have life, and that*
> *they might have it more abundantly.*
>
> John 10:10

Jesus came to give us abundant life, but the devil comes to steal, kill, and destroy. Since Satan is the author of sin, when we yield to it, we're yielding to him.

Again, the number one reason a born-again believer doesn't live in sin is because it's not our nature to do so now. If you knew this truth, you'd live holier accidentally than you ever have on purpose. You'd begin to understand that holiness doesn't make God move in your life, but a lack of holiness will give Satan access to you—which you don't want. God may still love you, but you'll be trying to run the race all weighted down. If you're dragging a hundred extra pounds, you might not even finish the race. That's the way it is with sin.

The Effects of Sin

Technically, you could go live in sin. But what would that do? Would it make God reject you? No. But it might make you reject God because it'll harden your heart. Hebrews 3:13 says that your heart can become hardened "through the deceitfulness of sin." Sin will slow you down. Satan will put problems in your life. Sickness and disease can come upon you through living in sin. Jesus told that to certain people, as the impotent (sick) man at the pool of Bethesda to whom He said, "Sin no more, lest a worse thing come unto thee" (John 5:14).

Some sickness—but not all—is related to sin. For instance, you could go live in adultery and God would still love you, but you will have opened up a huge door into your life for the devil, sexually transmitted diseases, emotional wounds, and a whole bunch of other things to come upon you. God would still love you the same, but sin will take its toll on your life.

Certain large media ministers went out and lived in sexual immorality and misappropriated funds, among other things. It's possible that these people were truly born again and really loved God, but they just got caught up in sin. I don't know their hearts, but if that's true, then God still loves them based on grace. But the devil made sure they paid dearly for their sin.

These are powerful truths, but they're so contrary to the way people think today!

They lost their ministries and their families. It cost them respect and honor. In some cases, they've had to spend time in jail. They've suffered ridicule and shame, guilt and condemnation. Although that sin hurt them tremendously, it's not God administering "punishment." They gave place to the devil, who then came in and stripped them. Satan is the one who caused them such grief and agony.

Servant of Righteousness

I am free *from* sin, but not *to* sin. Anyone who understands the Gospel isn't going to just go live in sin.

> *The grace of God that bringeth salvation hath appeared to all men, teaching us that, denying ungodliness and worldly lusts, we should live soberly, righteously, and godly, in this present world.*

> Titus 2:11,12

God's grace teaches us to live a holy life. Grace doesn't lead people into sin. Somebody might say, "Yeah, but I know this one person who heard about grace and then went and lived in sin." Not everyone who has heard the message of grace is going to be perfect. In the same way, not every person who has heard the message of guilt and condemnation is perfect. Either way, we're going to fall and come short at times. But the grace of God will ultimately break the dominion of sin if it's truly understood. People who comprehend and receive God's grace aren't emboldened to sin, but rather are freed from sin. These are powerful truths, but they're so contrary to the way people think today!

> *God be thanked, that ye were the servants of sin, but ye have obeyed from the heart that form of doctrine which was delivered you.*
>
> Romans 6:17

We were bound, like a slave, to that old nature. But now, through Jesus, we've been delivered.

> *Being then made free from sin, ye became the servants of righteousness. I speak after the manner of men because of the infirmity of your flesh: for as ye have yielded your members servants to uncleanness and to iniquity unto iniquity; even so now yield your members servants to righteousness unto holiness.*
>
> Romans 6:18,19

Whatever we've done, we need to see ourselves clean and forgiven through Christ.

Paul was saying, "I'm giving you an earthly example so you can better understand. In the same way that you were a slave to your old nature and sin, you need to see yourself now as a slave to your new nature and holiness. Recognize the truth and start seeing yourself righteous and holy in Christ. In the same way that this old attitude produced uncleanness in your life, this new attitude will produce holiness in your life if you could just see that your old nature is now dead and gone. If you could just understand how clean and pure you really are now in God's sight, you wouldn't go out and live in sin."

How Do You See Yourself?

One reason some people live in sexual immorality is because they see themselves as corrupted and defiled. They aren't seeing themselves as pure. They could break free if they ever understood that through Jesus they've been cleansed.

I was ministering to a woman once along these lines. She struggled with sexual immorality, but not all of it had been her choice. Some of it was rape, incest, and things like that. She felt defiled. So because she saw herself as defiled—even from when she was a little girl—it became like a self-fulfilling prophecy in her life. She was going out and reliving this defilement by giving in to sexual immorality.

While praying for her, the Lord gave me a picture to share with her. He told me to tell her that He saw her in the spirit clean and pure—just like a bride in total white and completely virginal. I started sharing these things with her for the purpose of letting her see herself that way. If she received this view of herself, it would break this dominion of sin.

When a woman sees herself as a prostitute, it becomes a self-fulfilling prophecy. Whatever we've done, we need to see ourselves clean and forgiven through Christ. If we can see that, there's no way we'll take the members of Christ—this holiness God has given us—and just go prostitute it again. This is the point Paul was making.

Just like a lost person's good actions cannot change their sin nature, neither can a born-again believer's sinful actions change their righteous nature.

"Free from Sin"

When ye were the servants of sin, ye were free from righteousness.

Romans 6:20

Before you were born again, you were a slave to that old sin nature. No matter how good you acted or how much you limited actions of sin, it didn't change your unholy nature. You were "free from righteousness." That didn't mean that before you were born again you couldn't do anything right. That's not the case. Some lost people are very good people. It just meant that all your righteous acts couldn't change your nature. You were by nature a child of the devil. (Eph. 2:3.)

What fruit had ye then in those things whereof ye are now ashamed? for the end of those things is death.

Romans 6:21

Back when you were letting your sin nature dominate and control you, there was a lot of fruit—sinful actions and all the death that came with them.

> *Now being made free from sin, and become servants to God, ye have your fruit unto holiness, and the end ever-lasting life.*
>
> Romans 6:22

When you were lost, you were a servant to sin (v. 20). Now that you're born again, you're a servant of God (v. 22). The sin nature is now dead and gone, and you have a brand-new spirit. Being "free from righteousness" (v. 20) means that as a lost person you could do some right things, but you couldn't change your sinful nature. Being "free from sin" (v. 22) means just the opposite—that even though you can commit some sinful actions, you cannot change your righteous nature. Did you get that?

Actions Don't Change Your Nature

Of course, a Christian can commit acts of sin. Many scriptures talk about this. But what Paul was saying is that just like a lost person's good actions cannot change their sin nature, neither can a born-again believer's sinful actions change their righteous nature.

Many Christians have accepted one side of this truth, but not the other. They know that someone's sinful nature cannot be changed just by doing good. But then, sad to say, they think that they can change and defile their born-again righteous nature by their actions of sin. This passage of scripture refutes this inconsistency. No more can you defile your born-again righteous nature by your acts of sin than you could perfect your sin nature by your acts of righteousness. If your acts of righteousness as a lost person couldn't change your sinful nature, then neither can your acts of sin as a Christian change your righteous nature. That's awesome!

I know this is raising many valid questions like, "Is this saying that when we sin, we don't lose our salvation?" I don't have space to adequately answer that here. So I recommend to you my teachings, "Security of the Believer" and "Complete Forgiveness," in addition to the one I've already mentioned entitled "Identity in Christ." This is a powerful, powerful truth!

"Well, Andrew, I understand that I was dead in sin up until being born again. I can also believe that I received a brand-new, righteous nature the moment I was saved. But I've sinned since then and my nature is corrupted once again." Wrong! Your nature doesn't become corrupted every time you sin any more than your nature became righteous every time you did something holy before you were born again. That's what these verses are communicating.

> In our born-again
> spirit, we are as
> Jesus is right now.

Romans 6:22 goes on to say, "Ye have your fruit unto holiness." Holiness is a fruit of salvation, not a root of salvation. Holiness is a by-product of relationship with God, not a way to obtain it. Holiness doesn't earn us anything from God. It's just the natural result of understanding our right standing with Him.

We've been corrupted through thinking things contrary to the Gospel. If we could just break free from a performance mentality to truly understand God's grace, we'd wind up living holier accidentally than we ever have on purpose. Once we're born again, it's just our nature to start living holy!

CHAPTER 10

Desiring Purity

Behold, what manner of love the Father hath bestowed upon us, that we should be called the sons of God: therefore the world knoweth us not, because it knew him not. Beloved, now are we the sons of God, and it doth not yet appear what we shall be: but we know that, when he shall appear, we shall be like him; for we shall see him as he is.

1 John 3:1,2

In our born-again spirit, we are as Jesus is right now. (1 John 4:17.) But when Jesus returns, we will become like Him in our minds and bodies.

Every man that hath this hope in him purifieth himself, even as he [Jesus] is pure.

1 John 3:3

This third verse is saying that every person who is truly born again has this inner drive for purity. You may not be fulfilling that drive very well—but it's there. Living under the law and its performance mentality will actually strengthen and empower the body of sin in your life. But if you're out from under the law, then:

> *Sin shall not have dominion over you: for ye are not under the law, but under grace.*
>
> Romans 6:14

As you start truly understanding grace—the Gospel, the power of God—it'll break the dominion of sin in your life and bring the benefits of salvation. If you are truly born again and understand grace, you'll manifest holiness. Deep down, you'll desire to fulfill your inner drive for purity.

> As long as you're in a performance mentality, you cannot experience intimacy with God.

Anyone who takes what I'm teaching here and says, "Well then, this frees me up to go live in sin," needs to be born again. If you were truly born again, you'd be seeking to purify yourself even as He is pure. You may be doing a poor job of it due to lack of understanding, but you desire to live for God.

Most people believe that our desire is just inherently evil. That's true of someone who isn't born again, and it can also apply to a born-again person whose mind isn't yet renewed. Their mind will continue to function in the corruption that it was programmed with from before until it's renewed. But if you were truly born again, you have a new drive on the inside of you. To the degree that you submit to and allow that new nature to dominate you, it'll start purifying your actions. That's when you'll find out—by personal experience—that the dominion of sin has been broken in your life.

Gift or Wages?

The wages of sin is death.

Romans 6:23

Wages speak of payment for something. When you have a sin nature, it produces—earns—death in your life. This isn't just referring to eternal death and being separated from God forever in hell. This also includes every effect of sin in this present life—depression, sickness, poverty, disease, anger, bitterness, unbelief, to name a few. Anything that's a result of sin is death and causes separation from God. Sin produced these negative effects in our life.

The gift of God is eternal life through Jesus Christ our Lord.

Romans 6:23

Eternal life is knowing God. (John 17:3.) It's not only just living forever, although that's a part of it. Paul was referring to an intimate, close, personal relationship with the Lord. If you

> I never had joy as long as I trusted my own holiness.

truly understand grace—the gift of God—then you can experience intimacy with Him through the Lord Jesus Christ. As long as you're in a performance mentality, you cannot experience intimacy with God. Regardless of how well you perform, it's always going to fall short. Eternal life—intimacy with Him—is a gift!

My Separated Life

Many people hear these things I'm saying and think I'm totally wrong because they've been so thoroughly indoctrinated in performance mentality. They reason, "This guy must be preaching this so he can justify an unholy lifestyle. It's just a way for him to excuse his sin. He's advocating sin."

Wrong! I could prove to you by my lifestyle that I'm not encouraging sin. I'm living holier than most of the people who would ever criticize me. I've never taken a drink of liquor or smoked a cigarette in all my life. I have never used profanity, nor even tasted coffee in all my life. Now I'm not saying that coffee and booze are the same thing. There's actually scripture you can stand on to drink coffee:

> *If they drink any deadly thing, it shall not hurt them.*
>
> Mark 16:18

That was a joke, by the way. But seriously, I've lived a super holy life. I'm living a separated life. Don't get me wrong, I'm not boasting in it and it's certainly not what I'm using as the basis of my relationship with God. I share this to counter those who would criticize me, saying, "You're teaching grace so you can advocate an ungodly lifestyle." No, grace hasn't caused me to go live in sin.

I'm living holier than many people have ever thought about living. Yet, I can tell you that I didn't have peace with God until I started understanding His grace. I was living a super holy life, but I never had peace as long as my faith was in my performance. I never had joy as long as I trusted my own holiness. God's power didn't flow in my life. Even though I might have lived better than someone else because of the choices I made, I still came short of God's perfect standard. Due to this, I never had boldness or confidence. But once I began understanding that I received from God by grace through faith, then I started experiencing real victory in my life. I found a holiness that was infinitely greater than mine.

> Once you comprehend how clean and pure you are through Jesus, you won't want to go live in sin.

Trusting His Righteousness

As long as I trusted in my righteousness, Satan could condemn me. He'd say,

"You aren't worthy!" and I'd try to argue with him that I was. Regardless of how much I'd done, he always won the argument. Why? Because there was always something I was failing in and something I wasn't doing.

But now that I've changed over to receiving from God through Jesus' righteousness, Satan doesn't win those arguments anymore. When he comes to me and says, "You aren't worthy!" I just agree with him, answering, "You're right. I'm not worthy. So I think I'll get it through who Jesus is. I'm going to pray in the name of Jesus, and because of His righteousness and His holiness, I expect to receive!"

Satan can't discredit the righteousness of Jesus. He could constantly discredit mine because it was only partial and always limited. But then I started trusting in the righteousness of God—a righteousness that came as a gift. (Rom. 6:23.) As I began believing and receiving it as a gift—receiving the Gospel, the good news—then power started operating in my life.

The Gospel is the power of God, but does this mean that we just go live in sin? God forbid! That's not what Paul was saying, and it's not what I am saying. You now have a brand-new nature. You're dead to sin. And once your mind is renewed and you really understand the true Gospel, you'll live holier accidentally than you ever did on purpose. Once you comprehend how clean and pure you are through Jesus, you won't want to go live in sin. It's just a matter of wisdom. Why give Satan an inroad into your life?

I don't want to give the devil any free shots at me. That's why I live as holy as I possibly can. It limits his inroads into my life. But I don't trust in that holiness for my relationship—right standing—with God. I trust in His mercy and grace. Ultimately, that's what grants me favor with Him.

It's in Your Spirit

It took me over twenty years to learn these things I'm sharing with you. These truths have revolutionized my life. They are some of the most profound things anyone could learn.

Even though you're born again, are you struggling with depression, discouragement, or other problems? You've asked the Lord into your heart and you know you're saved, but you haven't seen yourself dead to sin, dead to sickness, and dead to poverty. You still see yourself as a sinner, sick, and poor.

I've changed. I know now that I'm not the sinner trying to become holy. I am the righteous whom Satan is trying to make unholy. I'm not the sick trying to get well. I am the well that the devil is trying to make sick. I'm not the poor trying to be

> I'm fighting from a position of victory, not trying to get to one.

prosperous. I am the prosperous that the Enemy is trying to make poor. This is a totally different attitude and mindset. But I've found it much easier to fight from the position of victory than to try to fight to obtain a position of victory. It's infinitely easier to release something I already have than to go get something I don't.

You're headed for defeat if you're praying, "I am so unworthy and ungodly, but with God's help I believe I can attain unto righteousness." You might improve your actions, but you can't obtain that. You ought to say, "I'm so ungodly and helpless that I can't save myself. I just receive it as a gift. Because of Jesus, I'm now righteous through Him. I'm going to walk in righteousness, but not because it's something I'm trying to reach out for. It's something I'm releasing. I'm releasing the righteousness that's already in my born-again spirit."

There's doubt in the mindset that says, "I don't yet have it so I'm going to try to get it." You're starting from a position of defeat when you say, "I'm sick right now, but I'm going to seek God and get healed." No, the truth is: "In Jesus, I'm already healed. In my born-again spirit, I'm already well. I have the same power that raised Jesus Christ from the dead living inside me. (Rom. 8:11.) I'm dead to sickness and disease. I'm healed. It's in my spirit."

Renew, Release, and Experience

Do I deny that my flesh sometimes has sickness and other things come against it? No, I'm not denying that those things exist. Sometimes my body hurts, but I am denying its right and ability to dominate me. I know that in my spirit I'm dead to those things. I am risen with Christ. In the same way that He's far above all sickness, disease, poverty, and depression, so is my born-again spirit.

I'm in the process of renewing my mind so I can think like Christ. I arm myself with this same mind (1 Pet. 4:1); I let this mind be in me, which was in Christ Jesus. (Phil. 2:5.) I reckon myself to be dead to sin, but alive to God through Christ Jesus my Lord. (Rom. 6:11.) I'm fighting from a position of victory, not trying to get to one. My born-again spirit is as changed as it will ever be throughout eternity. The rest of the Christian life is just renewing my mind to what is already a reality in my spirit.

Sin's dominion over you has been broken. You are now dead to sin and alive to God. As you renew your mind to this truth, you'll start experiencing it in your everyday life.

CHAPTER 11

You Are What You Think

Although Romans 7 contains some familiar passages of scripture, they're usually misinterpreted. Due to this, most people already have a mindset and prejudice about what these verses really say. However, what it says and what people think it says are often worlds apart. Therefore, I encourage you to open your heart to the Lord so He can minister to you these truths from His Word.

> *That which I do I allow not: for what I would, that do I not; but what I hate, that do I. If then I do that which I would not, I consent unto the law that it is good. Now then it is no more I that do it, but sin that dwelleth in me. For I know that in me (that is, in my flesh,) dwelleth no good thing: for to will is present with me; but how to perform that which is good I find not. For the good that I would I do not: but the evil which I would not, that I do. Now if I do that I would not, it is no more I that do it, but sin that dwelleth in me. I find then a law, that, when I would do good, evil is present with me. For I delight in the law of God after the inward man: But I*

see another law in my members, warring against the law of my mind, and bringing me into captivity to the law of sin which is in my members. O wretched man that I am! who shall deliver me from the body of this death? I thank God through Jesus Christ our Lord.

Romans 7:15-25

There are usually three main reactions to this passage:

What in the world does this mean?

Frustration is normal in the Christian life.

Paul was describing himself before being born again.

The Impossible Life

Some people read Romans 7 and wonder, *What on earth was Paul talking about?* However, most people interpret this passage to say, "Frustration is normal in the Christian life." They argue, "The Apostle Paul—the man God used to write over half the New Testament—was mightily used of God. He wrote this as a mature believer after following Jesus for many years. Therefore, if he expressed such frustration in his Christian walk, then we shouldn't expect our experience to be any better. It doesn't matter how mature in Jesus you get, frustration is normal as a believer. There's a part of you that's bad and a part of you that's good. Sometimes you're good and sometimes you're bad. You'll always have this frustration of doing what you don't want to do and not being able to do the good that you do want to do. We're just like Paul. We want to do good, but it's just not in us. It's just a fact of life, so live with it. Adjust!"

A few people interpret this passage as Paul describing his life before being born

> The Christian life isn't just hard to live— it's impossible!

again. They reason, "Well, this couldn't be the same man who the Lord used to write most of the New Testament, work extraordinary miracles, plant churches, and turn the world right-side up. He couldn't have been talking about himself and how his Christian life was. So he must have been speaking about before he was born again, confessing, "O wretched man that I am!" (v. 24).

Of these three main reactions to this passage of scripture, none is right. Paul wasn't talking about frustration being a normal part of the Christian life. He wasn't referring back to before he was born again, either. He was describing the utter impossibility of succeeding in the Christian life through willpower. Paul was contrasting natural human ability (Rom. 7) with the intervention and power of the Holy Spirit. (Rom. 8.)

Notice how the word "spirit" is mentioned only once in all of Romans 7. But in chapter 8 (which we'll cover later on), it's mentioned twenty-one times. What an awesome contrast!

Romans 7 shows the impossibility of living for God. Most people don't understand this. They think that when you're

> Not enough Christians have ever experienced the consistent life of Jesus living through them.

born again, God forgives you and then picks you up, winds you up, points you in the right direction, and says, "Now let's see if you can do it right this time." They sing songs about God giving them a new start and another chance. However, this isn't truly descriptive of the Christian life. If it were, you'd blow it the second time just as much as you blew it the first. That's not victory. That's not true joy. That's not true liberty and deliverance. The Christian life isn't just you receiving another chance and now you're going to "live for God."

An Exchanged Life

The Christian life isn't just hard to live—it's impossible! It's humanly impossible to love your neighbor as you love yourself. Yet you'll hear people say, "Well, God commanded me to do it, so I'm trying." When someone spits on you or slaps your face, it's *humanly* impossible to turn the other cheek. You can't do that in your flesh. You don't have the natural ability to pray for those who despitefully use you, and turn around to bless and do good to them. (Matt. 5:44.) You don't have the ability to give your overcoat to someone who just took your coat from you in court. (Matt. 5:40.) You can't do it. Your flesh must be crucified so that Christ can live through you. (Gal. 2:20.)

The Christian life isn't a *changed* life, but an *exchanged* life. It's not where God comes in and now you have the ability to live for Him. You must learn to totally deny yourself, have no confidence in the flesh, and constantly become more dependent on Him. For instance, instead of gritting your teeth and trying in your flesh to say, "I'm going to love this person!" you'll pray, "Father, I choose to deny myself. You love them through me." Then just relax and let God's love flow out of you. Instead of saying, "Well, I'm never going to be discouraged or depressed again," you'll go to the Lord and pray, "Father, this person hurt me, but I praise You that You love me. I choose to meditate on that and let Your love flow through me to them." Just let Jesus start living through you.

Not enough Christians have ever experienced the consistent life of Jesus living through them. Many believers are busy trying to live for Him. Does that describe you? You do your best until you come to the end of your human ability and then cry out, "God, help!" Wrong! That's why people get into so many problems. We aren't supposed to do that.

It's not a matter of doing your own thing and praying, "God, please bless this endeavor. I want to dedicate it to You." That's the wrong attitude. You should say, "Father, what's

> You're trying to live for God, but it's you doing it in human strength rather than God living through you.

Your will for me? What's Your plan? I don't have any plans, any agenda of my own. I'm willing to be a street cleaner, dig ditches, or be a missionary to some faraway land. Father, I don't care what Your will is—here I am." When you reach that place of yieldedness to Him, He'll tell you what He wants you to do. Then, as you do what God tells you to do, it won't be you doing it, but the Lord doing it through you. You'll never have to ask Him to bless an endeavor if you're simply doing what He's commanded you to do.

But we're busy doing our own thing, living our own life in our own power. We're out there living in the lust of the flesh—buying things on impulse and putting ourselves in debt. Then we work our fingers to the bone, stressed out to the max, creditors hovering over us like vultures.

After we've done all these things it's pressure, pressure, pressure. Then we go to the Lord and say, "Oh, God, I'm claiming Your peace." The trouble is, you aren't going to have peace living a lifestyle that's totally against everything God says. You can't just sow all bad seed in your garden and then, when you see the weeds coming up, pray, "Oh, God, I'm asking You for a miracle—turn those weeds into corn!" It doesn't work that way.

Weak in Him

Although we blame him for a lot, the truth is that very little of what happens in our life is the devil. Of course, Satan is involved in everything negative. But all he has to do is tempt you and you'll ruin your own life. Many Christians are doing "spiritual warfare," binding the devil, rebuking this, and rebuking that. Yet the fact is that you're just reaping what you've sown.

Many believers haven't seen the devil or a demon in years. He doesn't have to come around. You're doing a perfect job ruining your own life. He taught you how to think and act, and you've run with it from there—with good intentions. You're trying to live for God, but it's you doing it in human strength rather than God living through you.

That's what Paul was showing us in Romans 7. On his own, he couldn't live the way he wanted to. In your flesh—your natural, human state—you can't live a perfect life. It's been said *Christian* means "little Christ." How can you be a little Christ in your flesh? You can't. You can't live like Jesus. You must come to Him, ask Him to live in and through you, and then learn to deny yourself.

> Many Christians still see themselves as a sinner saved by grace.

I called a woman on the telephone once and asked, "How are you doing?" She answered, "I'm weak in Him." At first,

I wondered, *Well, what does that mean?* But after she hung up and I pondered it some more, I thought, *That's pretty good!* She was saying, "I'm learning how not to trust in myself, but to recognize my weakness and let Him live through me." Instead of doing her own thing and then turning to God only when she gets in trouble, she was learning how to deny herself and just do what she felt God was leading her to do. That's what Paul described in Romans 7 and 8.

Change Your Thinking, Change Your Life

Let's go back to the beginning of Romans 7. Paul had been discussing the Gospel—how God loves us independent of our performance. He had used the first five chapters to make that point. Abraham and David were Old Testament examples. Past, present, and even future tense sin was all forgiven. (Rom. 4:7-8.) Therefore, sin was no longer the problem.

That raised the question, "Well then, what are you saying? Does this mean I can just go live in sin?" God forbid! (Rom. 6:2). "Why not?" It's no longer your nature to sin and you don't want to open a door to the devil in your life.

Many Christians still see themselves as a sinner saved by grace. If your concept of yourself is a forgiven, but still corrupt, sinner, then you cannot consistently perform contrary to the way you see yourself. You act the way you think of yourself in your heart. (Prov. 23:7.)

> You can tell what you've been thinking by what you're reaping.

If you see yourself as a loser, you'll eventually be a loser. You may know scriptures that describe how Jesus became poor so that you might be made rich. (2 Cor. 8:9; 9:8.) You may be aware of individual facts about prosperity, but if you see yourself as poor, you'll be poor.

Statistics consistently show that the vast majority of those who win the lottery soon end up in the same situation as before — or worse. Why? They didn't change their thinking. They didn't establish a wealthy image of themselves in their heart. Therefore, whatever caused them to get into the financial condition they were in before they won the lottery — if left unchanged — rises up and brings them again to the same place they were before. Unless you change your thinking, you'll stay the way you are.

The Garden of Your Heart

You are — right now — the way you have thought. If you're poor, you've been thinking poor. If you're sick, you've been thinking sick. If you're depressed, you've been thinking depressed. If you're angry and bitter, you've been thinking angry and bitter. Thoughts are seeds that take root in the garden of your heart and manifest themselves over time in your life.

To be carnally minded is death; but to be spiritually minded is life and peace.

Romans 8:6

Carnal mindedness is death. It doesn't just tend toward death. It's not one of the leading causes or contributing factors toward death. Carnal mindedness equals death.

But spiritual mindedness is life and peace. It doesn't just tend toward life. It's not one of the leading causes or contributing factors toward peace. Spiritual mindedness equals life and peace.

> We've been conditioned to be a certain way.

You can tell what you've been thinking by what you're reaping. If you aren't reaping life and peace, then you haven't been spiritually minded (or Word minded).

It's not politically correct to be absolute and dogmatic about anything in our society today. However, God's Word clearly reveals that you are what you've been thinking.

You Aren't a Victim

If you aren't prospering and succeeding, then it's because you've lost the battle in your mind. It's not circumstances. You aren't the victim. Today's "victim mentality" whines, "It's not my fault! It's society. I didn't get enough education. It's the welfare system. I came from a dysfunctional family. They ought to give me more money. If they (anyone and everyone else) would just treat me better, things would be fine!"

Everyone had a dysfunctional family. Yet some people with wrong thinking make excuses like, "I didn't get a puppy when I was a kid. That's the reason why I raped, murdered, and plundered. I didn't get what I wanted for my birthday. It's my parents' fault!"

We don't take responsibility for and control our own emotions. So we say, "It's a chemical imbalance. My hormones make me act like the devil one or two days a month." We blame anything and everything.

Thirty years ago most guys missed a mid-life crisis because they just didn't know about it. But today, we're so educated on it that everybody seems to go through one.

One of the reasons why Adam and Eve lived to be 930 years old is because they didn't know there was a "flu season." Nobody had "educated" them on the ten signs of a heart attack. Nobody told them that at thirty they were "over the hill." Nobody gave them black balloons and planted these seeds of death in them when they turned forty. They didn't know how to be victims. They'd never seen anyone die. Their son had been killed, but they didn't know how to die. They didn't know how to act badly, so they lived 930 years. We've been conditioned to be a certain way.

Wall-to-Wall Holy Ghost

If you see yourself as an "old man," it'll kill you. If you see yourself as a sinner—forgiven, saved by grace, but still a sinner by nature—you'll act like it. If you don't understand who you really are now in Christ, you won't experience His life and peace.

Remember that (non)gospel song I mentioned earlier that says, "I'm only human, I'm just a man… One day at a time, sweet Jesus, that's all I'm asking of You"? That kind of song will kill you. I'm not just human. I'm not just a man. One-third of me is wall-to-wall Holy Ghost. One-third of me is already renewed. I'm a new creature!

> As [Jesus] *is, so are we in this world.*
>
> 1 John 4:17

I am identical to Jesus in my born-again spirit because it's the Spirit of the Lord Jesus Christ that has been sent into my heart, crying "Abba Father!"

> *Now if any man have not the Spirit of Christ, he is none of his.*
>
> Romans 8:9

You aren't born again if you don't have the Spirit of Christ in you. If you have the Spirit of Christ in you, then you aren't an old man anymore. Your body and soul stayed the same, but the core of your being—the real you—is brand-new. You're a new creature. Old things have passed away. All things have become new. (2 Cor. 5:17.)

You must recognize that you're dead. The old sin nature that drove and compelled you toward sin is dead. It doesn't exist. It's the computer between your ears that your old man programmed that's causing you to continue to function that way. And it will until you reprogram it through the renewing of your mind.

> The pressures melt you, but you get to pick what mold you'll fit into.

It's Your Choice

I beseech you therefore, brethren, by the mercies of God, that ye present your bodies a living sacrifice, holy, acceptable unto God, which is your reasonable service. And be not conformed to this world: but be ye transformed by the renewing of your mind, that ye may prove what is that good, and acceptable, and perfect, will of God.

Romans 12:1,2

My definition of *conformed* is "to pour into the mold." The pressures of this life will melt you, but you'll fit into the mold that you choose. It's your choice what those pressures will do to you. It's not your upbringing, or your problems. It's not the terrible situations that have made you the way you are. If that were true, then everyone who has had the same problems you've had would have the same negative results. But it's not true. Some people who grow up with alcoholism in their home become alcoholics and others become teetotalers. The pressures melt you, but you get to pick what mold you'll fit into.

Don't be poured into the mold of this world, "but be ye transformed."

Transformed means "to change," like a metamorphosis.[1] How do you change like a caterpillar becomes a butterfly? "By the renewing of your mind" (Rom. 12:2).

Your born-again spirit has already changed. In your spirit, you're as perfect as you'll ever get. The only thing stopping you from experiencing the life of God within you is your brain. As you think, that's how you'll be. You can have the life of God within you and never experience it because of your head. Your unrenewed mind prevents you from enjoying God's peace, joy, and deliverance.

If you ever found out who you are in Christ, you'd live holier accidentally than you ever have on purpose. You need to understand that you are a new creature. It's not your nature to sin. It's the nature of a Christian to be holy. God has changed your "want to."

In your spirit, you're complete. But you also have a body and a soul. If you yield to Satan, he'll come to your emotional, mental, and physical realm to destroy you. Don't give the Enemy inroads of sin, sickness, poverty, or anything else. Renew your mind and keep the door closed to Satan!

CHAPTER 12

Your New Husband

Having made all the before mentioned points, Paul began speaking to Christians who used to be under the old Jewish law. They were very aware of God's standard of performance and judgment on sin.

> Know ye not, brethren, (for I speak to them that know the law,) how that the law hath dominion over a man as long as he liveth? For the woman which hath an husband is bound by the law to her husband so long as he liveth; but if the husband be dead, she is loosed from the law of her husband. So then if, while her husband liveth, she be married to another man, she shall be called an adulteress: but if her husband be dead, she is free from that law; so that she is no adulteress, though she be married to another man.
>
> Romans 7:1-3

Paul was drawing a comparison from the natural realm. It's a parable, like Jesus taught.

In this passage Paul was comparing our old nature and our new born-again nature. Once a couple is married, the spouse can't go out and have an intimate relationship with another person. They are bound—by law—to that mate. How do they get out of it? Although some people think they can just get a divorce, the only scriptural way to be released from the law of marriage is by the spouse's death. If the mate dies, then the marriage relationship is over and they're free to marry again. That's the point Paul was making.

Feel the Spirit?

Wherefore, my brethren, ye also are become dead to the law by the body of Christ; that ye should be married to another, even to him who is raised from the dead, that we should bring forth fruit unto God.

Romans 7:4

I'd like to take a moment and explain this comparison. You are made up of a spirit, soul, and body. The body is what you see in the mirror. Your soul is your intellect, emotions, will, and personality. Most people think the soul is the real you. They're unaware of the inner man—the spirit. They don't know the spirit exists. Or if they intellectually acknowledge it, they never—as far as experience goes—are able to discern what's spirit and what's flesh (body and soul).

Jesus answered.... That which is born of the flesh is flesh; and that which is born of the Spirit is spirit.

John 3:5,6

Whenever your soul comes into agreement and joins in your spirit's rejoicing, you'll praise God.

In other words, you can't "feel the spirit." We use that terminology, but technically, you can't physically sense the spirit. What you feel is when your soul gets into faith and the effects that it has.

For instance, if I were to speak to you about the promises of God, the fact that He is here, and that He has angels surrounding you right now, you'd begin to feel the presence of the Lord. Sometimes you can actually feel goose bumps and other sensations, but you aren't feeling the spirit. You're feeling the effect of your faith. The spirit cannot be felt.

Technically, you can't "dance in the spirit" either. If the spirit had control of you and possessed you, you'd dance better than you do. We wouldn't do this little charismatic two-step. Am I saying, "You're in the flesh"? No, not in the sense that it's carnal or wrong. But it's like Mary, who said:

My soul doth magnify the Lord, and my spirit hath rejoiced in God my Saviour.

Luke 1:46,47

In the Spirit

Your spirit is always rejoicing. It's always praising God. It's never depressed or defeated. And whenever your soul gets turned on to this, you can dance and it's not inappropriate. Whenever your soul comes into agreement and joins in your spirit's rejoicing, you'll praise God. There's nothing wrong with you praising God, but it's you—body, soul, and spirit— dancing, shouting, and praising the Lord.

> When you do what God's Word says, you're in the spirit.

Some people think that speaking in tongues is the Holy Spirit just taking control of you and speaking through you. It's not. God's Word says that "they… began to speak with other tongues, as the Spirit gave them utterance" (Acts 2:4).

It's like God speaking through me when I preach. He inspires what I say, but I'm the one saying it. He speaks to people through the words I say, but if I were to stand up before an audience and pray, "Oh, God, take my mouth and don't let me say one word of my own," and then wait until He "made" me talk, nothing would happen. God doesn't do that. It's Andrew Wommack talking, but the Holy Spirit is inspiring it.

The Holy Spirit doesn't "make" you dance. He's not going to grab hold of you and drive you up and down the aisle. If you're waiting for God to do that, it won't happen. You must realize that your spirit is jumping up and down on the inside and so you must—by faith—decide to jump up and down on the outside some too. That's being "in the spirit," but it's not the Spirit taking control of you.

Some people are waiting until the Holy Spirit just makes them throw their hands up in the air because they've never done it before. "Well, I just don't feel led." You old carnal thing! The Bible says to "lift up your hands in the sanctuary" (Ps. 134:2). When you do what God's Word says, you're in the spirit. Since your spirit is always praising God, it's always appropriate for you to lift your hands to worship Him. You don't have to wait on the Holy Spirit to grab you and make you do it.

You don't wait on the Holy Spirit to make you speak in tongues, either. You talk in tongues and the Holy Spirit gives you the utterance. It's your spirit that prays, not the Holy Spirit. (1 Cor. 14:14.) He inspires your spirit, but you're the one who does the praying.

The Tyrant Died

Your self—what you call "the real you"—is your soul. In Paul's comparison (Rom. 7:1-4), that self is the woman in the marriage. The reason why your self did the things it did before you were born again was because it was married to the corrupt old man—your sin nature.

> God couldn't give you a new nature as long as your old man was alive.

This sin nature was the nature of the devil. (Eph. 2:1-3.) We "were by nature the children of wrath" (v. 3). You were born into this world with a dead spirit—an old man—a nature that was against God. Your self—your soul—was married to this old nature, which dominated and controlled you. Your mind, will, and emotions were married to this old nature and you couldn't get separated. Just like a married couple, there was no way out, except by death. But this old guy wouldn't die—and he was a tyrant!

So how did you break free? When Jesus came and died for you, He took your old man—your sin nature—into Himself.

Know ye not, that so many of us as were baptized into Jesus Christ were baptized into his death?

Romans 6:3

You are dead in Him.

I am crucified with Christ: nevertheless I live; yet not I, but Christ liveth in me.

Galatians 2:20

Your old man died with Christ. Somehow, Jesus was able to take your sin—not your individual sins only, but your sin nature, your old man. Jesus literally took your sin nature upon Himself when He died. Now your sin nature is dead. It's gone—nonexistent.

Wed to the New Nature

This freed you up to be married to someone else: "That ye should be married to another, even to him who is raised from the dead" (Rom. 7:4). Although it's true that we are the bride of Christ and married to Him, in context this is referring to our self—our soul—being married to our new nature—our born-again spirit. Through Jesus, that old nature you were married to died, and now you have a brand-new, resurrected nature on the inside of you that you're married to. This new nature can now be your master the way your old nature used to be. This is what Paul was talking about.

However, most Christians don't understand this. They still feel wed to their old nature. They've perverted this so much that they believe we have a new born-again nature and an old sin nature, both living on the inside of us at the same time. We see ourselves as schizophrenic, and it's not true. It would be bigamy for us to be married to both an old nature and a new nature at the same time. That can't happen!

God couldn't give you a new nature (husband) as long as your old man was alive. So what did He do? He made a way, through His Son Jesus, for the old man to die; Paul described it in Romans 6:3 and Galatians 2:20. The old nature is dead and gone. Now you're married to a new man. You don't have a dual nature. You may still feel the effects of the old nature in you because he taught you how to think and act. (And remember,

You cannot
consistently
perform contrary
to the way you see
yourself to be.

you'll keep thinking and acting like him—even though he's gone—until you renew your mind.) But the truth is, you have a new husband!

Think of someone who's been married to a tyrant. They were hateful and did terrible things to their spouse. Then they died and the wife remarried. She's going to have the same thought patterns and actions toward her new husband as she did with her old. Until she renews her mind, she'll expect this present mate to treat her the same way as her previous mate.

I've dealt with many people who are destroying their second or third marriage because of prior relationships. They can't renew their mind to their new spouse. In the sexual relationship, they bring their old habits into a born-again marriage and cause lots of problems. Although that old mate is gone, they still retain the knowledge of what went on—and it affects their present relationship.

Emancipated!

That's the way it is with us. Our old man is gone. A part of you is not the devil anymore. That part is dead and gone. But you still have a mind that remembers all that junk. Since most of us don't understand that the old man is gone and we're wed now to a new husband, we see that we still have these thoughts and assume we're still the same old person. We think that there's still a part of us that is bent on doing wrong and we identify with it.

You cannot consistently perform contrary to the way you see yourself to be. (Prov. 23:7.) How do you see yourself? That's the way you're going to be. Do you see yourself as a loser trying to win? You're going to lose. Do you see yourself as a winner that Satan's trying to make lose? You'll win. There's a huge difference! Do you see yourself as the sick trying to believe God for healing? You'll be sick. Do you see yourself as the healed that Satan is trying to steal health from? You'll be well. Do you see yourself poor trying to become prosperous? You'll be poor. Do you see yourself as the prosperous—already done through Christ Jesus—that the devil is trying to hinder? You'll be prosperous. You have to get it on the inside before you get it on the outside. Everything you receive from God comes on the inside first.

You need to recognize that you are dead to this old man. He's gone. You aren't enslaved anymore—so stop acting like it. Imagine a woman whose husband would never let her come to church, never allow her to spend any money, and never let her

> We've been set free from sin, but many of us aren't free because we don't know what has happened.

out of the house. He just dominated and controlled her. Then one day he dies and she marries another fellow. Even though this new husband is the best she could have ever hoped for, if she doesn't renew her mind, she'll continue acting trapped. She'll reason, "I just know my husband won't let me go to church. I can't spend any money. I just have to stay here cooped up in this house all the time!" She'll live in bondage—even though she's free—until she changes her thought patterns to be in accordance with her new man.

We saw earlier that President Lincoln set the slaves in America free when he issued the Emancipation Proclamation and how it's a documented fact that many still lived in slavery. Their masters didn't show them the proclamation and they didn't have access to news the way we do today. It was often years before they found out. These people spent extra time in slavery, being free. Since they didn't know it, they just continued serving that old master.

We've been set free from sin, but many of us aren't free because we don't know what has happened. We're still serving that old master. This is the comparison Paul was making.

CHAPTER 13

The Schoolmaster

When we were in the flesh, the motions of sins, which were by the law, did work in our members to bring forth fruit unto death.

Romans 7:5

Remembering that *sin* here—as in most of Romans—is a noun[1] in the original Greek, we can better understand what Paul was saying. Before we were born again, our sin nature—strengthened by the law—motivated and compelled us to do sinful actions, "Now we are delivered from the law, that being dead wherein we were held" (Rom. 7:6).

What's dead? Our old man—he was the part held under the law. The law governed and ruled our old sin nature. The law was given only for people with sin natures.

You can lust only for something that's forbidden.

Knowing this, that the law is not made for a righteous man.

1 Timothy 1:9

Notice this verse says, "The law is not made for a righteous man." Who is righteous? Anyone who's born again. Therefore, the law was never made for a Christian. It was for a lost person, someone who had an old man. The law governed our old man, but it doesn't govern our new man. There is no law against our new nature because it doesn't have any propensity or ability to sin. (Gal. 5:22-24.)

> *When we were in the flesh* [before we were born again], *the motions of sins, which were by the law, did work in our members to bring forth fruit unto death* [our sin nature—the part of us governed by the law—compelled us toward sinful actions]. *But now we are delivered from the law, that being dead wherein we were held* [now we're free from the law because our sin nature is dead]; *that we should serve in newness of spirit, and not in the oldness of the letter. What shall we say then? Is the law sin? God forbid.*
>
> Romans 7:5-7

My teaching entitled *The True Nature of God*[2] goes into much more detail. I'm only going to be able to briefly summarize it here.

"Bless God, I Shall!"

> *Is the law sin? God forbid. Nay, I had not known sin, but by the law: for I had not known lust, except the law had said, Thou shalt not covet.*
>
> Romans 7:7

"Thou shalt not…" all of a sudden lust came alive. That's what Romans 7:7-8 is saying: "I wouldn't even have known what lust was if the law hadn't told me not to covet. But the moment the commandment came, lust came alive."

Until the Commandment Comes

Sin, [took] occasion by the commandment.

Romans 7:8

The commandment facilitated sin. It didn't help you overcome it. The commandment helped sin overcome you. It helped your sin nature to dominate and control you. The Old Testament law won't set you free from sin, but it'll actually make sin dominate you.

Sin, taking occasion by the commandment, wrought in me all manner of concupiscence [desire or lust]. *For without the law sin was dead.*

Romans 7:8

What a radical statement! Remember, this isn't talking about the actions of sin, but rather the sin nature. Your sin nature was powerless. It wasn't dead in the sense that it didn't exist. It was present, but impotent. Your sin nature didn't exercise any real dominance or control until the commandment came.

This is why a child can be sweet, innocent, sensitive to God, and have Him speak to them before they're actually born again. It's not because they came to earth with a pure nature. They were born with a sin nature too. It's just that sin isn't imputed to them until the commandment comes. (Rom. 5:13.)

Sin Revived

I was alive without the law once: but when the command-ment came, sin revived, and I died.

Romans 7:9

Notice the word *revived*. It didn't say that sin came. Sin revived. That sin nature was already in all of us, but it lies dormant until the time the law comes. Then sin revives and we die.

What Paul was talking about when the commandment comes is what many of us call "the age of accountability." There's a time when you are real young that you may do things that are wrong. You may know that you're going to get in trouble if you do something, but there comes a time when it goes beyond just, "I'm going to get spanked if I do this." You realize that you're not just disobeying Mom, Dad, or society, but you're rebelling against God. The moment you reach that point, then the commandment has come. You've reached the age of accountability.

> The law was given
> to take away our
> hope of ever
> saving ourselves.

This age varies. Some folks—like those who are mentally retarded—may never reach an age of accountability. Even though they were born with a sin nature, if they were to die in that state, sin wouldn't be imputed against them. That's why when a child dies they don't go to hell if they weren't old enough to be born again. That sin nature isn't imputed to them until the law comes. But there comes a time in our life when we pass the threshold of innocence and willfully rebel against God. At that moment, sin revives and we die. The law was given to make this happen.

Our sins had already defeated us. We already had a corrupt nature, but we were comparing ourselves among ourselves, thinking, *Well, I'm okay. Surely God will accept me.* (2 Cor. 10:12.) The Lord had to shake us out of this deception. "Do you think you're okay? Just because you've murdered only one person instead of ten doesn't make you good." God had to tell us that this wasn't right. So He shook us out of our complacency by showing us a standard that was so holy, perfect, and pure that no one could keep it.

The law strengthens sin. (1 Cor. 15:56.) It didn't strengthen us in our battle against sin. It strengthened sin—our sin nature—in its battle against us. The law was given to make sin come alive on the inside of us. Then we realize, "Oh, God, I didn't know I had this stuff in me!"

To Bring Us to Christ

Before faith came, we were kept under the law, shut up unto the faith which should afterwards be revealed. Wherefore the law was our schoolmaster to bring us unto Christ, that we might be justified by faith.

Galatians 3:23,24

The law was given to take away our hope of ever saving ourselves. It was designed to show us our corruption and cause us to run to God, crying, "Help! I need a Savior!" But through supernatural demonic influence, religion has turned the law around from being something that condemns and kills to something that "gives life" (2 Cor. 3:6–7,9): "Oh, thank You, God, for showing me all the steps that I must do." Through subtlety, religion has enticed us to embrace the law. Although it was good in the sense that it showed us our need for God and drove us to Him, the law cannot produce salvation. (Rom. 3:19-20.) If there could have been a law given which would have produced life, then righteousness would have come by it. (Gal. 3:21.) But the law has concluded (enclosed or declared) all under sin. (Gal. 3:22.) It's bound all of us up and shown us our need of a Savior.

The commandment, which was ordained to life, I found to be unto death.

Romans 7:10

The commandment itself was perfect and holy, but the problem was none of us were. Even though it could have given life if we would have kept the law in its entirety, it actually produced death because only one person in all of history has ever kept the whole law—and it wasn't you or me.

Your Old Man Is Dead

Sin, taking occasion by the commandment, deceived me, and by it slew me. Wherefore the law is holy, and the commandment holy, and just, and good. Was then that which is good made death unto me? God forbid. But sin, that it might appear sin, working death in me by that which is good; that sin by the commandment might become exceeding sinful.

Romans 7:11-13

The purpose of the command was to make us despair of ever saving ourselves. It brings the knowledge of sin, condemnation, and guilt, and makes us say, "I'm such a sinner. I'll never make it on my own!"

That's also why most Christians are so condemned and guilt-ridden today. They're still trying to relate to God on the basis of their performance. God never gave the law to show us all the things we had to do so we could get straight. Instead, He was willing to relate to us through mercy and grace. But mankind was taking God's lack of punishment upon sin as approval. They were deceived, so God finally had to say, "All right, you think you're good enough. Here's what I demand." Then He gave them a standard that nobody could keep.

Paul was saying that the law was for ruling our old man, who's now dead: "I have a new man on the inside. Now I'm free from the law. Just like a woman who was treated badly in her marriage doesn't have to fear a dead husband, my old nature is gone. It's over with. Because of my new mate—my born-again spirit—I don't have to feel guilty anymore." Christians shouldn't feel guilty or condemned anymore because that old man—which the law governed—is now dead, gone, and nonexistent.

> We must have this brand-new man on the inside of us and we must let him be the one to live through us.

Let the New Man Live

We know that the law is spiritual: but I am carnal, sold under sin.

Romans 7:14

In other words, "The law is perfect, and I'm not. So the law and I could never get along."

That which I do I allow not.

Romans 7:15

> If you'll let this brand-new spirit live through you, there is no condemnation, no judgment, no sentence against you.

This brings us back to Romans 7:15-25. In essence, Paul was saying, "In the natural, just me by myself, I can't do anything. I can't save myself. I had to become a new person through God's gift of regeneration. It had to be His work, because I couldn't change my nature. I couldn't get out of this situation. God had to kill my old man and give me a new one." Paul wasn't crying, "I'm schizophrenic! Sometimes I do good, sometimes I do bad. I just can't help myself." He was simply describing the inability of any of us on our own to live for God. We must have this brand-new man on the inside of us and we must let him be the one to live through us.

CHAPTER 14

In and After the Spirit

At the end of Romans 7, Paul said, "O wretched man that I am! who shall deliver me from the body of this death? I thank God through Jesus Christ our Lord" (Rom. 7:24-25).

Notice that he didn't say, "I thank God *for* Jesus Christ our Lord." He was saying, "I thank God I'm delivered from the body of this death *through* Jesus Christ our Lord." In other words, Paul was describing the futility of trying to serve God in the flesh. The flesh part of us (body and soul) will always fall short. "Imperfection can't be perfect. How do I ever get out of this? Praise God, through Jesus Christ our Lord, I have a brand-new person inside of me."

Then Paul moved right into chapter 8, which speaks of letting our born-again spirit dominate our lives through the power of the Holy Spirit. Romans 7 describes frustration, defeat, and sin coming alive. Romans 8 overflows with victory. As I said earlier, the Spirit/spirit is mentioned once in chapter 7, and twenty-one times in chapter 8. Paul was contrasting Christ living through us (Rom. 8) with our trying to live for God. (Rom. 7.) That's powerful!

Free from Condemnation

There is therefore now no condemnation to them which are in Christ Jesus.

Romans 8:1

Who is in Christ Jesus? You are if you've been born again and have this new man. With this new nature, there is no condemnation to you when you are in Christ Jesus and walking "not after the flesh, but after the Spirit" (v. 1).

If you'll let this brand-new spirit live through you, there is no condemnation, no judgment, no sentence against you. Nothing can stop you. Nothing can hold you down. This born-again man doesn't have any limitations or inadequacies. As Jesus is, so are you in your spirit. (1 Cor. 6:17; 1 John 4:17.)

Condemnation refers to declaring unfit for use. When you condemn a building, you declare it unfit for use. The devil does that to you by saying, "You sorry thing. What makes you think God would use you?" That's condemnation.

The law of the Spirit of life in Christ Jesus hath made me free from the law of sin and death.

Romans 8:2

The law that governed my old man declared, "You're a loser and a failure. You can't lay hands on the sick and see them recover. You can't prosper. You can't be happy. You can't have joy." That old man is now dead and gone. The law that enforced his rule isn't over me anymore.

> What the [Old Testament] law could not do, in that it was weak through the flesh, God sending his own Son in the likeness of sinful flesh, and for sin, condemned sin in the flesh.
>
> Romans 8:3

If I would not have been imperfect, the Old Testament law would have been great. I would have kept it and that would have solved the problem. But because I was imperfect, through my flesh, the Old Testament law—instead of being something good—actually became my condemnation. So God sent His own Son as a man, and judged sin in His flesh.

Positional and Experiential

> That the righteousness of the law might be fulfilled in us, who walk not after the flesh, but after the Spirit. For they that are after the flesh do mind the things of the flesh; but they that are after the Spirit the things of the Spirit.
>
> Romans 8:4,5

How can you tell if you're walking after the Spirit or after the flesh?

There's a difference between "in the flesh" and "after the flesh," and "in the Spirit" and "after the Spirit."

If you are born again, you are *in* the Spirit. That's a positional truth. It's the way you are. But you might not be walking *after* the Spirit. You might be walking after the flesh and letting your physical self dominate, which means you won't experience in the natural realm the victory that's yours in the Spirit. But the truth is—positionally—you're in the Spirit.

If you aren't born again, you are *in* the flesh. That's your position. But you could walk *after* the Spirit. In other words, you could imitate the things of the Spirit. Although you could do some right things, it won't change your standing with God. Only being born again can do that.

In speaks of your position in Christ (in the Spirit) or not (in the flesh). This is consistent all the way through this eighth chapter of Romans. However, *after* speaks of how you are experiencing things.

What Are You Thinking?

*They that are after the flesh **do mind** the things of the flesh; but they that are after the Spirit the things of the Spirit.*

Romans 8:5

How can you tell if you're walking after the Spirit or after the flesh? What are your thoughts focused on? Are they on the flesh? Is your mind occupied with fear, strife, depression, or poverty? Then you're after the flesh. If you're after the Spirit, you'll be thinking about God. You'll be meditating on His Word and who you are in Christ. It's really that simple!

> *To be carnally minded is death; but to be spiritually minded is life and peace.*
>
> Romans 8:6

If you're thinking on carnal things, you're after the flesh. For instance, if someone treats you badly and you mull it over again and again, you'll be hurt, depressed, and offended. That's what carnal mindedness produces—death. It's not so much what that person did to you that made you angry, bitter, and upset. It's the fact that you meditated and thought on it that empowered it in your life.

I've had people come against me, but I've learned to be quick to cast things over onto the Lord. I refuse to think on the negative side of things. There are people who have promised to kill me if I ever set foot on their property. There are nationwide ministers—people you'd know if I named them—who believe that I'm the slickest cultist since Jim Jones.[1] They've even proclaimed that publicly. People have used my tapes to criticize me. But do you know what? I don't think on those things. And as a result, I'm not hurt or offended. I've held meetings and

> You have this new spirit on the inside of you and the only thing holding you back is your "stinkin' thinkin'".

been on the exact same platform as some of these folks. I've loved them. I've sent people to their churches and given offerings toward their projects. I speak nothing but well of them. I'm not angry or bitter because I don't dwell on those things.

It's not what people do to you that makes you angry, but how you think about it. If you're carnally minded, you'll get carnal results. If you're spiritually minded, you'll get spiritual results. This is awesome!

You Are Not in the Flesh

The carnal mind is enmity against God: for it is not subject to the law of God, neither indeed can be. So then they that are in the flesh cannot please God.

Romans 8:7,8

Lost people cannot please God. They are *in* the flesh. They aren't born again. They don't have the life of God inside them. They have this old sin nature instead. For them, it's impossible to please God.

Ye are not in the flesh....

Romans 8:9

If you're born again, you aren't *in* the flesh. You're *in* the Spirit. You may be walking *after* the flesh and getting the same results as you did before being born again. But the truth is, you aren't *in* the flesh anymore.

> [You are] *in the Spirit, if so be that the Spirit of God dwell in you. Now if any man have not the Spirit of Christ, he is none of his.*
>
> Romans 8:9

And we could go on and on. There are some powerful truths here, but it's basically saying that you're already free in Christ. You have this new spirit on the inside of you and the only thing holding you back is your "stinkin' thinkin'". You still think like you're married to that old man. "Well, I resisted for a while, but I'm just an old sinner after all. I'm going to sin anyway, so I might as well give in now." If you think that way, you're walking in the flesh and you'll reap corruption.

Here's what you need to begin to realize: "I'm free. There's nothing in me that's making me defeated. There's nothing in me that can make me depressed. No outside circumstances can make me discouraged. My spirit is always full of love, joy, peace, longsuffering, gentleness, goodness, faith, meekness, and temperance. (Gal. 5:22-23.) I have a choice. Will I let hurt, depression, anger, and bitterness rule me? Or will I be spiritually minded and let who I am in Christ reign? It's my choice." If you think that way, you'll be

Turn from self-reliance, self-salvation, and self-righteousness.

walking in the Spirit and you'll be free to receive God's blessings and goodness. Now that's freedom!

CHAPTER 15

The Righteousness of God

Romans 7 isn't the normal Christian life. It's the frustration of the person trying to serve God out of their own human ability. They could be either non-Christian or born again. But the flesh—our self—is incapable of ever living the victorious life God intended for us.

Romans 8 shows us the Spirit-filled life. It's describing the person who has understood the power of the Gospel and is letting the Spirit of God live through them.

The entire book of Romans reverberates with the message of God's grace. Turn from self-reliance, self-salvation, and self-righteousness. Accept God's free gift of righteousness and salvation by faith in the Gospel. Live by faith in God's grace!

Paul began Romans 9 lamenting the fact that the Jewish people were trusting in their own righteousness to produce salvation. He spoke of his deep longing for his natural brothers (Paul himself was a Jew) to be saved. Instead of receiving the

> The grace of God is offensive to religious folks!

free gift of God through Jesus, they were trying to earn salvation. They didn't want to come and be dependent on Christ, the Savior. They were trusting in their own goodness instead.

Then Paul shifted gears by saying, "Well, it's not a total loss. A true Jew isn't just a physical, natural-born Jew, but those who are the true children of the promise—who walk with the faith of Abraham." Again, this brings up some very offensive things to these religious people.

Righteous Heathen?

At the end of Romans 9, Paul made a summary of the things he'd said thus far and transitioned into chapter 10:

> *What shall we say then? That the Gentiles, which followed not after righteousness, have attained to righteousness, even the righteousness which is of faith. But Israel, which followed after the law of righteousness, hath not attained to the law of righteousness.*
>
> Romans 9:30,31

We just don't understand how radical this statement was to the people Paul was writing to in his day. He was talking to people who were very zealous in keeping the law. (Rom. 10:2.) Their entire life was built around seeking God. The law influenced how they dressed, what they ate, their politics, their work schedule, and their giving, among other things. At certain times of the day, everybody stopped to pray. These were religious people. Their whole life was consumed with seeking God.

Then Paul came along and thoroughly rattled their religious cage by saying that the Gentiles had received by faith what the Jews were working so hard to attain by their actions. A *Gentile* is a non-Jew, but the term in Paul's day had become synonymous with a pagan. They were people who had no relationship with God. Instead of denying themselves, they indulged themselves. We'd call them *heathen* today. Yet Paul was saying, "These heathen—who weren't following after righteousness, who weren't seeking God, who weren't trying to live holy— have attained unto righteousness by faith" (v. 30).

If that wasn't bad enough to the Jews, put it together with verse 31, "But Israel—all you religious people trusting in your performance for salvation—have not attained unto it," and is it any wonder that Paul upset the religious people wherever he went? He was saying, "These heathen out here that weren't even trying to live holy are more acceptable to God than you. They have become righteous by faith in the Gospel and you who were living holy are rejected by God." This incensed many people.

It was probably why Paul suffered the persecution that he did, and it's the reason why anyone who preaches the true

> They are putting their faith in their actions instead of receiving salvation as a gift.

Gospel of God still suffers persecution even today. (Gal. 5:11; 6:12.) The grace of God is offensive to religious folks!

The Stumblingstone

Wherefore? [Why? Why is this true? How could this be?] *Because they* [the religious Jews] *sought it* [righteousness] *not by faith, but as it were by the works of the law. For they stumbled at that stumblingstone.*

Romans 9:32

The reason why the nonreligious have become accepted by God and the religious remain rejected is because the non-religious sought righteousness by faith in God's grace and the religious sought it by faith in their own holy actions.

When the heathen heard the Gospel—that salvation was a gift and they didn't have to earn it—they embraced it. To them, it was very beneficial because they hadn't been living a proper life and they knew it. When someone came along and told them that God would accept them on the basis of grace as a gift, and that all they had to do was believe and receive Jesus as their Savior, they went for it. What a deal!

The religious person rejected Jesus for basically the same reasons—the Gospel told them it wasn't their goodness that earned them relationship with God. They had to believe on Jesus and receive salvation as a gift. They responded, "That's not fair! Look how hard I've worked. I've put a lot of effort into this. Do you mean that all of my self-denial doesn't make God love me more? Are you saying that all of my holy living doesn't make me any better than the person who's been living in gross sin? Do you mean that I need the same degree of salvation as this old reprobate over here?" Religious pride won't let them receive a free gift like that.

The exact same thing happens all around the world today. Many religious people are trying to do the right things—and it's not that what they're doing is wrong. It's the fact that they are putting their faith in their actions instead of receiving salvation as a gift. For these people, it's offensive to hear the Gospel preached. It's upsetting to listen to some-body say that someone could not be living as holy as they are, but receive from God better because they're putting faith in a Savior instead of earning it. Those are fighting words for a person who's trusting in themselves.

> We don't need justice—we need mercy

"It Just Isn't Fair!"

I've seen this happen again and again. Some pillar of the church is there every time the doors are open. They pray and lead a Sunday school class. They knit quilts and bake pies. They're always doing religious deeds. But they've been struggling for years with some sickness, financial need, or problem in their life that hasn't been met. Then some drunk comes in off the street with nothing to offer God. Someone tells them the Gospel, saying, "It's not according to how holy you are. You don't need a track record of righteousness. Just receive what you need from God as a gift. All you have to do is believe." This reprobate receives the same miracle that dear old saint so-and-so has been seeking for twenty years. The drunk gets it and the religious person doesn't. So the religious person swells up with pride and whines, "It just isn't fair!"

We don't need justice—we need mercy. I used to work in a photography studio developing pictures. We'd joke about some of the people who came in to look at their proofs. Often, they'd comment, "This picture doesn't do me justice." Although we never actually did it, we wanted to say, "Lady, you don't need justice. You need mercy!" If God gave us what we deserved, even dear old saint so-and-so wouldn't receive. We can't approach God based on faith in ourselves. We might think we deserve it more than someone else, but all have sinned and come short of God's standard. (Rom. 3:23.)

Religious people trusting in their own goodness are the hardest people to reach. They were the ones who gave Paul the biggest problems. They crucified Jesus and persecuted the church. It's still religious people today who come out against the true Gospel.

Good people trusting in their own holiness are the most difficult to reach with the Gospel of the Lord Jesus Christ. When the Gospel is preached to someone who isn't living righteous, it's good news. They respond in faith to that positive message of God's grace. But unless God supernaturally intervenes with revelation and conviction, a religious person trusting in their efforts will resist the Gospel. They're proud of what they've accomplished and they feel better than somebody else because of their own effort. The Gospel sounds to them like all their great righteousness has been to no avail.

Of course, holiness is still beneficial because it denies Satan access into our lives and helps us in our relationships with other people. But it doesn't make us more acceptable to God. Neither does our lack of holiness make us less acceptable to God. Our relationship with God must be based entirely upon faith.

Good Works, But Wrong Motive

Romans 9:32 says that these religious people didn't receive righteousness because they sought it not by faith but by the works of the law. *Works of the law* refers to doing good things, but with the wrong motive. It's trusting in what you have done instead of trusting in what God has done.

> Either you accept
> the truth and it
> becomes liberating
> and life-giving, or
> you deny it and it
> becomes damning.

The Bible also refers to *works of faith.* (1 Thess. 1:3; 2 Thess. 1:11.) The motive is the difference. A *work of the law* is when you're doing something with the mindset that this is going to earn you relationship with God. He owes it to you based on what you did. That's a work of the law. A *work of faith* may be the exact same action, but the mindset behind it is, "I'm not doing this to earn relationship with God, but because God has already given me relationship with Himself. I love Him and want to serve Him." Works of faith are motivated by faith and love, not a sense of obligation and debt.

Paul was saying that these Jews had the wrong motivation. They were doing the right things with the wrong motive. So they stumbled over the stumblingstone. (Rom. 9:32.) Then he quoted from Isaiah 8:14 and 28:16 of the Old Testament:

> *As it is written, Behold, I lay in Sion a stumblingstone and rock of offence: and whosoever believeth on him* [Jesus Christ] *shall not be ashamed.*
>
> Romans 9:33

In other words, Jesus Christ is planted right in the path of every single person. God confronts every individual with the truth that they need a Savior because they cannot save themselves. Some respond properly by faith and receive the Lord and His precious gift of salvation. Others try to maintain their own goodness and stumble over the grace of God. The very thing that caused them to trip over Jesus the Savior will make them fall flat on their faces on their way to hell—trusting their own holiness. Either you accept the truth and it becomes liberating and life-giving, or you deny it and it becomes damning. It's your choice.

Misdirected Zeal

In the next chapter, Paul repeated what he said at the beginning of Romans 9 about his fellow countrymen—the Jews:

> Brethren, my heart's desire and prayer to God for Israel is, that they might be saved. For I bear them record that they have a zeal of God, but not according to knowledge.
>
> Romans 10:1,2

These Jews were very zealous for God, but not according to knowledge, meaning they were spiritually blind—they were ignorant of their heavenly Father and of His Son.[1] In other words, having the right knowledge is more important than having the right actions.

These Jews were doing some great things. They were praying, paying tithes, and doing many of the commands within the law. A Pharisee—a religious Jew—would be accepted into any modern church today. They were prayer

You can lust only for something that's forbidden. In the sexual realm, do you lust for your spouse? We don't normally refer to it that way because if it's legal, then it's not lust. Lust is always referred to in an illicit, illegal manner. You don't lust for something you have, but for things you don't have. You never have lust until somebody puts a restriction on you.

Remember the earlier example of the kids spitting on the flower? It's the same thing. God originally created us without restrictions, so there's just something in us that resists them. When we hear, "Thou shalt not..." something on the inside answers, "Bless God, I shall!"

That's why God gave the law. It wasn't because we didn't have a clue about what to do and needed God's instructions—one through ten thousand—about how to get right with Him. The purpose of the law was for the person who was thinking, *I never do anything wrong. There's nothing wrong with me. I'm such a good person. God has to accept me. I'm better than this old publican over here. I fast twice a week and pay tithes of mint, anise, and cumin. I'm holy. God must love me!* (See Luke 18:9-14.) The law was for the self-righteous religious person who was lost and didn't know it.

God said, "You think you're righteous? You think you're good enough? Let Me show you My standard. Thou shalt not..." All of a sudden, this sin that was already present—this old nature—just rose up on the inside. When God declared, warriors, faithful attendees, and diligent tithers. Very few churches would ever deny membership to a diligent tither! These Pharisees were very holy people, but their zeal was for the letter and form of the law, and not for God Himself.[2] Due to that fact, they weren't accepted by God. They had misdirected zeal and knowledge.

Many people today say that it doesn't matter what you believe, as long as you believe something. They teach that there are many ways to God. It doesn't matter if you're a Buddhist, Hindu, Muslim, or Christian, in the end they all come together. Wrong! This mindset is in direct opposition to what Romans 10:2 is saying.

These religious people had a zeal for God—not just zeal, but zeal for God. However, it wasn't according to knowledge. Therefore, it wasn't a saving knowledge. They were sincere, but sincerely wrong. They believed the wrong thing.

Two Types of Righteousness

They being ignorant of God's righteousness, and going about to establish their own righteousness, have not submitted themselves unto the righteousness of God.

Romans 10:3

There are two different types of righteousness:

God's righteousness

Self-righteousness

> We don't become righteous gradually as we improve our actions.

We obtain self-righteousness by trusting in our own actions. We receive God's righteousness by faith in Jesus Christ. (Eph. 2:8-9.) So out of the two ways to righteousness, only one is correct. The only righteousness that will put us in right standing and relationship with God is the righteousness of God that is given to us as a free, unearned gift. Most people are seeking after a righteousness that comes based on their own works and performance. This is what Paul was saying about these Pharisees in Romans 10:3.

Sad to say, there are still many people today who are ignorant of God's righteousness. When you use the word *righteousness*, most people think about their own actions. They think about their own performance. If someone were to stand up in church and declare, "I'm righteous," they'd be criticized and reminded of things they'd done wrong. Most believers wouldn't think of their born-again spirit that has had God's righteousness imputed. They'd be looking on externals.

There are two different kinds of righteousness: the kind that we produce by our own actions and the kind that God gives us

You can't be self-dependent and God-dependent simultaneously.

when we're born again. The only kind of righteousness that we can relate to God on is the one that comes as a free gift. In our born-again spirit, we are the righteousness of God in Christ Jesus. (2 Cor. 5:21.)

Compared to the righteousness that comes from God, our self-righteousness is like a filthy, soiled rag. (Is. 64:6.) God's righteousness is infinitely more and our self-righteousness is infinitely less. The Jews were ignorant of God's righteousness, and so are most religious people today. They don't understand that we are made righteous the moment we place our faith in Jesus Christ. We don't become righteous gradually as we improve our actions. We're born again righteous—it's a gift!

CHAPTER 16

Grace and Works Don't Mix

*Of him are ye in Christ Jesus, who of God is made
unto us wisdom, and righteousness, and sanctification,
and redemption.*

1 Corinthians 1:30

When you believe on Christ, God sends forth the Spirit of
His Son into your heart and you become born again.

Therefore if any man be in Christ, he is a new creature.

2 Corinthians 5:17

Created Righteous

What is this new creature like? What is this brand-new,
born-again spirit like? Righteous!

*He hath made him to be sin for us, who knew no sin; that
we might be made the righteousness of God in him.*

2 Corinthians 5:21

God's righteousness has been imputed unto you. It's not just a little bit of righteousness either. Your new man is truly righteous.

> *Put on the new man, which after God is created in right-eousness and true holiness.*
>
> Ephesians 4:24

You don't become righteous through your own actions—you are created righteous. When you were born again, God gave you a righteous nature. But the sad thing is that most Christians are ignorant of this. They don't know their born-again spirit is righteous. They aren't aware of the truth that righteousness comes as a gift from God. So they try to maintain a righteousness based on actions, which can never be the basis of our relationship with God.

Mutually Exclusive

We just saw in Romans 10:3 that there are two types of right-eousness—God's righteousness and our own righteousness. They are mutually exclusive. You can't be trusting in righteous-ness as a gift through the Lord Jesus Christ and trusting in self-righteousness at the same time. You can't be self-dependent and God-dependent simultaneously. Someone who is trying to live a righteous life with the motive, "This righteousness that I do is going to earn me relationship with God," cannot also be trusting in the grace of God too. You're either relying on God's grace or yourself, but not a combination of both.

> *If by grace, then is it no more of works: otherwise grace is no more grace. But if it be of works, then is it no more grace: otherwise work is no more work.*
>
> Romans 11:6

God may treat you by grace, but people relate to you based on performance.

You're either trusting grace or works for salvation, but not a combination of the two. This verse debunks the perversion of the Gospel that says, "Yes, you need a Savior. Yes, Jesus died for you. But you can't be right with God through Jesus only. You need to maintain a minimum standard of holiness and then God makes up the difference." No! Either you're saved by grace or works, but not by a combination of the two. They simply do not mix.

Therefore, if you aren't submitted to God's righteousness—if you're trying to establish your own righteousness as the foundation of your relationship with God—then you aren't submitted unto the righteousness of God. You must be one way or the other.

Holiness Helps with People

Is it okay then to just live in sin? Of course not. You do benefit from maintaining a self-righteousness—your own actions of holiness. God doesn't receive and relate to you based on your self-righteousness. Your actions have nothing to do with His grace, His mercy, and His opinion toward you. It's totally unmerited and completely unearned. But you do need to maintain a righteousness in your own personal actions when it comes to relationship with other people. God may treat you by grace, but people relate to you based on performance.

> The Gospel will produce power in you to overcome sin and live a holy life.

Your employer doesn't hire you by grace. They don't say, "Hey, I understand God loves you no matter what you do. I'm a grace employer and I love you too. So whether you show up for work or not, I want you to know that you have a guaranteed position, cost-of-living raises, and retirement. There's nothing you can do that would make me fire you. You don't have to perform. It doesn't matter if you ever do anything. I just love you by grace!" No, that's not the way it is.

As far as your life experience here on earth goes, it's important that you perform well. If you have a boss, you need to serve them well. They will relate to and reward you based on your performance. Although it shouldn't be, marriage will likely be the same. We ought to be giving each other God's unconditional love, but the truth is that you aren't living with Mr. or Mrs. Perfect yet. Until they are perfect, they're probably going to judge you based on your performance. If you perform badly, then you'll suffer the consequences of it.

As a student, if you don't do the work or perform well on the test, you're going to suffer for it. If you don't perform well driving a car, you could kill yourself or someone else. Your actions do cost you something in relationship with other people—and Satan is always looking to take advantage of your actions in any way he can. Therefore, it's important to maintain good actions, but it's vital that you never misunderstand the reason for holiness and the actions that go along with it.

Holiness helps you in your relationship with people. It shuts the door on the devil and keeps him out of your life. But it is not the way God views you. He looks on your heart—your spirit man—not your outward appearance. He doesn't deal with you based on your external actions of righteousness. God relates to you based on the inner qualities of who you are in Christ. He deals with you totally by grace.

There is a purpose for godly actions, but it's not so you can put your faith in them for relationship with God. That's the whole issue. No one is saying that a Christian shouldn't be living holy. It's just a matter of where your faith is. Is your faith in your actions or in the Savior? If your faith is in the Savior, does that mean you won't have godly actions? No, if you truly understand and receive the Gospel, you'll live holier accidentally than you ever have on purpose. It'll just flow out of you.

> Remember, the law was not given for the purpose of our justification.

The Gospel will produce power in you to overcome sin and live a holy life. But it will be a fruit of salvation, not the root.

The Law Fulfilled

> *Christ is the end of the law for righteousness to every one that believeth.*
>
> Romans 10:4

End basically means "termination" here.[1] For believers, the law has fulfilled its purpose. It's no longer a way we pursue in order to try to obtain righteousness. In truth, the law was never given to produce right standing with God. It was given to show us how completely separated from Him we were. It was given to make the old sin nature rise up on the inside of us and overcome us. It was given to reveal to us our need for a Savior. When we turn from self to place our faith in Christ for salvation and to receive God's free gift of grace, the law then has accomplished what it was given to do. Anyone who truly understands the Gospel and what Jesus came to do will recognize that the law is now over for producing righteousness to everyone who will believe and receive righteousness as a gift.

"Well then, was there ever anyone who was made righteous through the law?" Yes, there was one person—the Lord Jesus

Christ. He came and fulfilled every precept of the law. Through doing that, He literally deserved right standing with God. He had it by His very nature. He obtained it through His actions. Therefore, Jesus had it by inheritance and by conquest. He obtained right standing with God through every means available.

> Burnout is nothing more than trying to produce the fruit of salvation through your own effort.

To Jesus, the law was a way to bring salvation not only to Him, but to everyone who would put faith in Him. But He's the only One who has ever kept the law. Nobody else has ever been justified by the law—and you and I aren't either. Remember, the law was not given for the purpose of our justification.

As Paul continued to write about righteousness, he began quoting Old Testament scripture about the law:

> *Moses describeth the righteousness which is of the law,*
> *that the man which doeth those things shall live by them.*
>
> Romans 10:5

This is talking about a person who is legalistic and trusting their own goodness as the foundation of their relationship with God. Due to this, they are consumed with doing. They live by their doing. That leads to the treadmill effect.

The Treadmill

When you start thinking that you are justified with God through your actions, you may be motivated and hopeful for a brief period of time. You might think, *Hey, I can live better than this and then God will accept me*. But it's a treadmill you can't get off.

In Shreveport, I tried to get some exercise once while running on a treadmill. Since I wanted a workout, I had that thing cranked up to nine miles per hour (which is a very fast pace). After awhile, the towel that I had put on my handlebars to wipe my face with fell. Not thinking, I bent over to pick it up. That treadmill kept right on going, knocked me flat on my back, and shot me ten or fifteen feet across the wooden gym floor. That's how I learned the hard way that once you're on a treadmill, you just can't stop! It's the same with trying to be justified by your actions.

Once you start trusting in your own holiness, it puts you under this burden and pressure to perform, and regardless of how much you do, you always could have performed better. This causes frustration and it's the reason Christians get exhausted. Burnout is nothing more than trying to produce the fruit of salvation through your own effort. It's legalism. But when you trust in God and His grace instead, you'll experience His strength, joy, and peace.

In context, this word translated *live* here in Romans 10:5 means "to continue to remain alive."[2] In order to live, you must do certain things to continue to remain alive. Once you start trusting in justification through the law, then you just have to start feeding this thing. You have to maintain this holiness that just isn't natural. Since you will make mistakes, when you do, you're going to bear the guilt and punishment that goes along with it.

A legalist is basically a perfectionist. They try to perfect this flesh, which isn't the system that God has set up. He's established becoming righteous through accepting it as a free gift based on what Jesus has done. Place your faith in Christ's performance, not your own.

A Legalistic Approach

The righteousness which is of faith speaketh on this wise, Say not in thine heart, Who shall ascend into heaven? (that is, to bring Christ down from above:) Or, Who shall descend into the deep? (that is, to bring up Christ again from the dead.)

Romans 10:6,7

How then does the righteousness that comes from God speak? Paul just talked about how the righteousness that is of the

Instead of demanding you to come up to Him, He's already come down to you.

law—a legalistic approach—is totally consumed with doing. It's work, work, work. It's a treadmill. It's tiring, frustrating, and impossible. Nobody can keep up.

So how does the proper way of receiving righteousness with God speak? Well, you don't have to say in your heart, "I must be so holy that I live like an angel here on the earth." You don't have to climb a ladder of perfection in order to ascend into heaven through your own holiness and good works. The Lord isn't demanding that you approach Him in heaven. He's not requiring you to become perfect and live up to His standard. Instead, Jesus came down to you and now offers righteousness as a gift.

Verse 6 is saying that you don't have to be so holy that you earn your way up to heaven. Christ has already come down and done everything He needed to do for you to become righteous. Verse 7 is saying that you don't have to do so much penance that you go to hell and bear the punishment for your own sin because Christ has already done that for you. Jesus has already descended into hell and literally bore your separation from God so that you don't have to bear it.

Do you see the point Paul was making in verses 6 and 7? It's not your great holiness that earns you relationship with God. Instead of demanding you to come up to Him, He's already come down to you. Instead of requiring you to do penance and suffer punishment for your sin, Jesus has already been separated from God and gone to hell for you.

Doing Penance

> Jesus has already taken your punishment and borne it for you.

I met a man in Arlington, Texas, once while ministering along these lines. Earlier in his life he had been under this deception of thinking that what Christ suffered for us wasn't enough. He actually thought he had to do penance too. He showed me the grotesque scars on his elbows and knees that he had received down in Mexico. During the week of Easter one year, he had crawled three miles over broken glass on his hands and knees to do penance. He told me that there were people who actually got up on a cross. Some were tied with rope and others were actually crucified. Their purpose was to try to bear the sufferings of Jesus and do penance for their sins.

Most of us would say, "That's foolish! There's no reason we must do that. Jesus has already paid that for us." That's true, but the devil has some other more subtle ways of enticing us into the very same thing. We all fail sometimes and sin against God. Instead of just trusting what the Scripture says about forgiveness, we still feel like we have to do penance. We must go through a few extra days bearing remorse until God will really forgive. Maybe we feel we must spend an extra hour reading the Word or praying, or we must give some extra in the offering to make up for the failure we had. There isn't anything wrong with extra study, prayer, or giving from the right motive.

But if your motivation is to do it as penance, then you are—in a sense—bringing Christ up from the dead. It's like He didn't go to hell and suffer your payment for you. You've got to suffer it. That's double jeopardy! Jesus has already taken your punishment and borne it for you. Therefore, you don't have to bear it again or add anything to it.

It's probably human nature to think, *Well certainly, I must suffer something. It just makes sense. I'm the one who has caused all this grief. How could Jesus suffer all of this for us?* The truth of the Gospel is that He did. Jesus has already borne your punishment and suffering for you. So now you don't have to ascend into heaven through your own holiness, and you don't have to go down into hell through penance and remorse. Just receive what God has already done.

Faith's Confession

> But what saith it? The word is nigh thee, even in thy mouth, and in thy heart: that is, the word of faith, which we preach.
>
> Romans 10:8

What do you do if you don't have to go up to heaven or down to hell in order to receive salvation and the free gift of grace? Simply confess the word of faith—that you have placed your faith in Jesus Christ as your Savior. Don't mix works and grace!

CHAPTER 17

Heart Belief and Mouth Confession

If thou shalt confess with thy mouth the Lord Jesus, and shalt believe in thine heart that God hath raised him from the dead, thou shalt be saved.

Romans 10:9

Salvation isn't based on your being holy. It's based on heart belief and mouth confession. This, of course, is much more than just saying some words. It's talking about a firm commitment, a complete reliance, and an absolute trust in Jesus Christ as your Lord and Master. You're dependent on Him for salvation. What a tremendous passage of scripture!

However, this verse has almost become a religious cliché. We've become so familiar with it that we don't understand its importance. But the religious people Paul wrote to understood.

This was totally contrary to the methods they taught for salvation. They taught a performance-based system of works. They had a rigorous schedule of holiness and observed all these rituals and laws. They were on a treadmill of work, work, work. Then Paul came along and preached, "All you have to do is make Jesus your Lord and believe in your heart that He's been raised from the dead. He'll live in you and you'll be saved. Just receive it by faith." This was radical to the Jews of that day.

It's still radical to a lot of people today! Many folks simply won't believe that it's just faith in Jesus alone that produces salvation. They also believe that they must be holy. But it's not what Paul was saying here.

> *With the heart man believeth unto righteousness; and with the mouth confession is made unto salvation.*
>
> Romans 10:10

It's heart belief and mouth confession. It's not just saying words. Many people today repeat what's called "The Sinner's Prayer," but they're just mouthing words. They are the right words, but unless they're coming from a heart of faith, it's just sounding brass and a tinkling cymbal. First you believe it in your heart. Then you speak it with your mouth. It's a combination of the two. There must be an outward profession on your part, but it works only once you have a heartfelt faith.

Zealous in Wales

Sometimes we've actually just gotten people to repeat after us without really first believing it in their heart. Our tour group in Wales was doing some street ministry. We were singing and a crowd gathered. Some of us were working among the crowd and sharing the Gospel with people. One fellow in our group was zealous. He witnessed to everything that moved! Although he had a good heart, he didn't exactly know the right way to do it.

As this fellow was talking to a woman who was standing right behind me, I listened to how he was presenting the Gospel. He was trying really hard to get her to pray this prayer with him. Finally, she gave in and said, "Okay."

> When you truly believe from your heart, God will never disappoint you.

"Now repeat after me: I confess with my mouth the Lord Jesus Christ…"

"I confess with my mouth the Lord Jesus Christ…"

"And I believe in my heart that God has raised Him from the dead…"

Pause… "I can't pray that."

"Why not?"

"Because I don't believe that Jesus is alive from the dead. I believe He was a historical figure, but not that He was raised from the dead. That's all just a lie."

So this young guy who was trying so hard to lead her to the Lord said, "Well, it doesn't matter what you believe. Just say this prayer after me and you'll be saved!"

I had to intervene and tell him, "No, this isn't the way you do it. According to the Word, it does matter what you believe in your heart. It's not just mouthing the words—even if they are the right words. It's with the heart that you believe and with the mouth that confession is made."

Stick with the Gospel

The scripture saith, Whosoever believeth on him shall not be ashamed.

Romans 10:11

When you truly believe from your heart, God will never disappoint you. He's faithful. If you confess with your mouth and believe in your heart, you will be saved.

This isn't talking only about the initial born-again experience. It also means everything that comes as a result of what Jesus Christ did—healing, deliverance, and prosperity. If you need healing in your body, all you have to do is confess with your mouth and believe in your heart, and according to the Bible, you'll be healed. If you've done that and haven't seen healing manifested, then somehow or another there's a deficiency in your faith. Stick with the Gospel, meditate on these things, and understand that God has already done it. You are dead to sin—and therefore dead to sickness and poverty. In your born-again spirit, you've already got your healing, financial provision, or whatever you are believing for. The moment your natural mind is renewed to the truth of God's Word, it will begin to manifest in the physical realm.

> In God's eyes, there is no difference between those who have lived a holy life and those who have committed many sins.

God has already provided—through the atonement of Christ—everything we'll ever need. Now it's up to us to believe and receive. My study of Ephesians entitled *You've Already Got It!* takes a closer look at this truth and reveals practical insight that will really facilitate and accelerate your receiving from God. Along with my teaching *Spirit, Soul & Body,* I believe that *You've Already Got It!*[1] contains some of the most helpful truths God has ever shown me. Without understanding these vital truths from God's Word, you won't be able to experience very much of what Jesus died to provide.

No Difference

There is no difference between the Jew [the religious zealot] *and the Greek* [the heathen]: *for the same Lord over all is rich unto all that call upon him.*

Romans 10:12

In God's eyes, there is no difference between those who have lived a holy life and those who have committed many sins. The same access to Him is granted on the basis of faith. The person who hasn't lived holy will have more problems in this life than the one who has. But as far as your relationship with God is concerned, the only way to Him for everyone is by grace through faith. It doesn't matter if you've lived holy or not, if you can release faith in what Jesus Christ has done, you can receive the benefits of salvation.

> *Whosoever shall call upon the name of the Lord shall*
> *be saved.*
>
> Romans 10:13

This is true for both the initial born-again experience and for the ongoing receiving for the rest of your life of everything Christ has provided for you through His death, burial, and resurrection. For whosoever shall call upon the name of the Lord, shall be forgiven, healed, delivered, prospered—every benefit that's ours through what Jesus Christ did comes to us by grace through faith.

Give Up the Treadmill

Paul also discussed these two different types of righteousness in Philippians 3. In essence he said, "Is anyone trusting in their own holy living for right standing with God? If anyone could, it should have been me. I was circumcised on the eighth day, born of the stock of Israel, of the tribe of Benjamin. No one was more Hebrew than I was! Concerning my knowledge and practice of the law, I was among the elite religious group known as the Pharisees. Our entire lives were consumed with legalistic obser-vation of the law. Concerning zeal, I actively hunted down and persecuted the followers of Jesus. I was blameless concerning the law. I may not have kept every precept, but it certainly wasn't because I didn't try. I gave it all I had. I ran that fleshly treadmill with all my heart." (Phil. 3:4-6.)

> Regardless of how good we could ever be, our holiness is still limited and imperfect.

What happened that caused Paul to give up the treadmill?

> *What things were gain to me, those I counted loss for Christ. Yea doubtless, and I count all things but loss for the excellency of the knowledge of Christ Jesus my Lord: for whom I have suffered the loss of all things, and do count them but dung, that I may win Christ.*
>
> Philippians 3:7,8

Paul was saying, "I had a standard of holiness that nobody could excel. No one was more zealous and diligent than I. But I gave it all up for Christ." Here is Paul's reason for giving up everything:

That I may win Christ, and be found in him, not having mine own righteousness, which is of the law, but that which is through the faith of Christ, the righteousness which is of God by faith.

Philippians 3:8,9

In this passage Paul was saying that the righteousness that comes through Jesus is infinitely greater than any righteousness he could have ever obtained on his own. Actually Paul said the same things in Philippians 3 as he did over in Romans 9 and 10. He gave up everything—all of his trust in his own goodness and holiness—so that he could be found in Christ. That meant not found with self-righteousness, but with a righteousness that came through Jesus—through faith in Him.

The righteousness God gives us at salvation is infinitely greater than any righteousness we could ever obtain on our own. Regardless of how good we could ever be, our holiness is still limited and imperfect. But the righteousness that comes from God through faith is perfect. It's His righteousness!

I may know him, and the power of his resurrection, and the fellowship of his sufferings, being made conformable unto his death; if by any means I might attain unto the resurrection of the dead.

Philippians 3:10,11

Paul was saying, "I had a standard of righteousness that exceeded any of my critics, but it didn't do me any good. I didn't have any real joy or peace in my life until I quit relying on myself and started trusting in God's righteousness. What keeps religious people from experiencing peace with God is the fact that in their hearts they're trusting in themselves. By doing so, they aren't submitted to the righteousness that comes from God."

Run Up the White Flag

These truths we've discussed in this brief synopsis of the book of Romans are still just as pertinent today as they were back when Paul wrote them. Our current religious system causes people to trust in their own goodness and performance for right relationship with God. We can never be good enough to have God owe us right standing. He has to give it to us as a gift. Nobody is good enough to earn relationship with God through their performance. The fact that we're trusting in our own performance is the very reason why Satan is able to defeat us.

> We just need to give up, run up the white flag of surrender, and start trusting in God's grace.

The devil doesn't come to us and criticize God's ability. He just tells us that the Lord won't use His power on our behalf because we are so sorry. So it's not really an issue of whether God has the ability, but rather it's His willingness to use His ability on our behalf. The reason why we doubt God's willingness is because we think that He moves in our life proportional to our performance. We're under a law mentality. Even though we're born again and not offering Old Testament sacrifices for our sin, receiving the mark of circumcision in our bodies, or praying three times a day, we still have the same mentality.

We're traveling down the same road to the same destination. All we've done is change vehicles. Instead of taking all of those Old Testament rules and regulations, we've picked out a few of them and added some more. Common vehicles today include being baptized a certain way, belonging to a certain church, reading your Bible an hour a day, being holy, not wearing jewelry, having your dress a certain length, piling your hair up on your head, and not wearing makeup, among others. You must do this and you can't do that.

If you're basing God's acceptance of you on any of your actions, then you aren't believing the Gospel. You may not think it's law because it isn't Jewish tradition, but it's still a law mentality. It's the same thing, just substituted with other elements.

That's the very reason why so many people are frustrated today. They aren't enjoying the peace and victory God brings. They haven't understood that salvation is a gift. Instead of trying so hard to do all these things, we just need to give up, run up the white flag of surrender, and start trusting in God's grace.

When you do that, Satan can't condemn you. There isn't any condemnation to those who are in Christ Jesus and walk after the Spirit. When you're born again and walking after the Spirit, you don't experience the frustration of trying to please God by your own effort. (Rom. 7-8.) Let the brand-new nature of your born-again spirit flow through you. (Gal. 2:20.) When you do, Jesus lives through you and you enjoy freedom. Nothing can condemn or successfully come against you.

There's a level of victory that most Christians have never attained because they are still so law minded and trying to please God by their own efforts. When they fail, Satan comes in and condemns them, saying, "You sorry thing! God won't do it because of you."

Mix with Faith

The Gospel dispels that deception. It brings us back to a place of recognizing that God hasn't had anybody who is qualified working for Him yet. He moves in our life because of mercy and grace, not justice. Once you understand that, God's love will abound in your heart more than ever before. Once you understand the Gospel, love comes. And once you understand God's love, your faith will work because faith works by love. (Gal. 5:6.)

How could you doubt the One who loved you so much that He gave His only Son for you while you were still a sinner?

> This understanding doesn't set you free *to* sin, but free *from* sin.

How much more does God love you now that you're born again? Even though you're still not everything you're supposed to be, you're His child and He loves you.

If you could accept the greatest of all miracles—the born-again experience—when you were a sinner, separated from God, nothing going good for you, now that you're born again how much more should you be able to see these small things like healings of disease, deliverance from demons, and miracles of provision? Those things pale in comparison to receiving the initial born-again experience!

If we could really understand this and start walking in God's grace, our faith would abound. Victory would follow and we'd find out that the Gospel truly is the power of God unto salvation to everyone who believes. But you must believe it. The Gospel doesn't produce automatically. It has to be mixed with faith.

> *Unto us was the gospel preached, as well as unto them: but the word preached did not profit them, not being mixed with faith in them that heard it.*
>
> Hebrews 4:2

We must know the Gospel, understand the Gospel, and believe the Gospel. Then that Word will profit us.

Father, I Love You!

I hope that this study through the book of Romans has really opened your eyes to the truth that God loves you independent of your performance. This understanding doesn't set you free *to* sin, but free *from* sin. As you understand God's goodness, sin's dominion over you is broken and you are led to repentance. I pray that God gives you revelation of this right now so that your mind can be renewed to this awesome spiritual reality. May these truths work in your life to the point that you are far more conscious of righteousness than you are of sin. (Heb. 10:2.)

In light of everything the Lord has just revealed to you about your relationship with Him, why don't you take a moment right now to pray?

"Father, I thank You for making me righteous by faith in Your Son. Thank You for giving me right standing with You as a free gift. Please help me to comprehend these truths more fully and to apply them to my daily life. I want to glorify You with holiness, but for the right reason. By faith, I receive these truths from Your Word into my heart. Thank You for being so good to me. I love You!"

Receive Jesus as Your Savior

Choosing to receive Jesus Christ as your Lord and Savior is the most important decision you'll ever make!

God's Word promises, "If thou shalt confess with thy mouth the Lord Jesus, and shalt believe in thine heart that God hath raised him from the dead, thou shalt be saved. For with the heart man believeth unto righteousness; and with the mouth confession is made unto salvation" (Rom. 10:9–10). "Whosoever shall call upon the name of the Lord shall be saved" (v. 13).

By His grace, God has already done everything to provide salvation. Your part is simply to believe and receive.

Pray out loud, "Jesus, I confess that You are my Lord and Savior. I believe in my heart that God raised You from the dead. By faith in Your Word, I receive salvation now. Thank You for saving me!"

The very moment you commit your life to Jesus Christ, the truth of His Word instantly comes to pass in your spirit. Now that you're born again, there's a brand-new you!

Receive the Holy Spirit

As His child, your loving heavenly Father wants to give you the supernatural power you need to live this new life.

> *Every one that asketh receiveth; and he that seeketh findeth; and to him that knocketh it shall be opened... If ye...know how to give good gifts unto your children: how much more shall your heavenly Father give the Holy Spirit to them that ask him?*
>
> Luke 11:10,13

All you have to do is ask, believe, and receive!

Pray, "Father, I recognize my need for Your power to live this new life. Please fill me with Your Holy Spirit. By faith, I receive it right now! Thank You for baptizing me. Holy Spirit, You are welcome in my life."

Congratulations! Now you're filled with God's supernatural power. Some syllables from a language you don't recognize will rise up from your heart to your mouth. (1 Cor. 14:14.) As you speak them out loud by faith, you're releasing God's power from within and building yourself up in the spirit. (1 Cor. 14:4.) You can do this whenever and wherever you like.

It doesn't really matter whether you felt anything or not when you prayed to receive the Lord and His Spirit. If you believed in your heart that you received, then God's Word promises you did. "Therefore I say unto you, What things soever ye desire, when ye pray, believe that ye receive them, and ye shall have them" (Mark 11:24). God always honors His Word; believe it!

Please contact me and let me know that you've prayed to receive Jesus as your Savior or to be filled with the Holy Spirit. I would like to rejoice with you and help you understand more fully what has taken place in your life. I'll send you a free gift that will help you understand and grow in your new relationship with the Lord. Welcome to your new life!

Endnotes

Chapter 1

[1] Based on information from *Baker's Evangelical Dictionary of Biblical Theology,* available from http://bible.crosswalk.com/ Dictionaries/BakersEvangelicalDictionary/bed.cgi?number=T395, s.v. "Judaizers."

[2] Thayer and Smith, *The KJV New Testament Greek Lexicon,* "Greek Lexicon entry for Euaggelion," available from http://www.biblestudytools.net/Lexicons/Greek/grk.cgi?number=2 098&version=kjv, s.v. "gospel."

[3] Ibid., "Greek Lexicon entry for Euaggelizo," available from http://www.biblestudytools.net/Lexicons/Greek/grk.cgi?number=2 097&version=kjv, s.v. "gospel."

[4] Ibid., "Greek Lexicon entry for Euaggelion," available from http://www.biblestudytools.net/Lexicons/Greek/grk.cgi?number=2 098&version=kjv, s.v. "gospel."

Chapter 2

[1] Based on information from Thayer and Smith, "Greek Lexicon entry for Sozo," available from http://www.biblestudytools.net/ Lexicons/Greek/grk.cgi?number=4982&version=kjv, s.v. "save."

Chapter 3

[1] *The True Nature of God* is available in book, tape, or CD form and can be ordered through my ministry at http://www.awmi.net/store, or through my contact information found at the end of this book.

Also, the MP3 audio files are available as free downloads at my website.

Chapter 4

[1] *Strongs's Exhaustive Concordance of the Bible,* #4318, available from http://www.eliyah.com/cgi-bin/strongs.cgi?file=greeklexicon&isindex=4318, s.v. "access" Romans 5:2.

Chapter 5

[1] *Spirit, Soul & Body* was one of the first revelations I received through studying the Bible. It has served as a foundation for almost everything the Lord has shown me since. These important truths freed me from the bondage of much wrong thinking and enabled me to consistently experience God's supernatural power. Personally, I cannot comprehend how anyone can truly prosper in their relationship with God apart from understanding this basic revelation. I've seen the Lord set more people free through *Spirit, Soul & Body* than almost anything else I've ever ministered. Check it out!

Chapter 7

[1] *Spirit, Soul & Body* is available in book, tape, or CD form and can be ordered through my ministry at http://www.awmi.net/store, or through my contact information found at the end of this book. Also, the MP3 audio files are available as free downloads at my website.

[2] Based on information from Thayer and Smith, "Greek Lexicon entry for Hamartia," available from http://www.biblestudytools.net/Lexicons/Greek/grk.cgi?number=266&version=kjv; based on information from "Greek Lexicon entry for Hamartema," available from http://www.biblestudytools.net/Lexicons/Greek/grk.cgi?number=265&version=kjv; and based on information from "Greek

Lexicon entry for Hamartano," available from <http://www.bible-studytools.net/Lexicons/Greek/grk.cgi?number=264&version=kjv>.

3 Ibid., "Greek Lexicon entry for Hamartia," available from http://www.biblestudytools.net/Lexicons/Greek/grk.cgi?number=266&version=kjv; and "Greek Lexicon entry for Hamartema," available from http://www.biblestudytools.net/Lexicons/Greek/grk.cgi?number=265&version=kjv;

Chapter 8

1 Thayer and Smith, "Greek Lexicon entry for Metamorphoo," available from http://www.biblestudytools.net/Lexicons/Greek/grk.cgi?number=3339&version=kjv, s.v. "transformed," Romans 12:2.

Chapter 11

1 Based on information from *Merriam-Webster's Collegiate Dictionary,* 11 ed. (Springfield, Massachusetts: Merriam-Webster, Inc., 2003), s.v. "transform."

Chapter 13

1 Thayer and Smith, "Greek Lexicon entry for Hamartia," available from http://www.biblestudytools.net/Lexicons/Greek/grk.cgi?number=266&version=kjv, s.v. "sins," Romans 7:5.

2 *The True Nature of God* is available in book, tape, or CD form and can be ordered through my ministry at http://www.awmi.net/store, or through my contact information found at the end of this book. Also, the MP3 audio files are available as free downloads at my website.

Chapter 14

1 Leader of the Peoples Temple cult that ended with a mass suicide of over 900 members, including Jones, in 1978.

Chapter 15

[1] Based on information from *The New John Gill's Exposition of the Entire Bible,* "Commentary on Romans 10:2," available from http://www.studylight.org/com/geb/view.cgi?book=ro&chapter=01 0&verse=002, s.v. "but not according to knowledge," Romans 10:2.

[2] Based on information from *Robertson's Word Pictures of the New Testament,* "Commentary on Romans 10:2," available from http://www.studylight.org/com/rwp/view.cgi?book=ro&chapter=01 0&verse=002, s.v. "but not according to knowledge," Romans 10:2.

Chapter 16

[1] Thayer and Smith, "Greek Lexicon entry for Telos," available from http://www.biblestudytools.net/Lexicons/Greek/grk.cgi?number=5 056&version=kjv, s.v. "end," Romans 10:4.

[2] Based on information from *Merriam-Webster,* s.v. "live."

Chapter 17

[1] *Spirit, Soul & Body,* and *You've Already Got It!* are available in book, tape, or CD form and can be ordered through my ministry at http://www.awmi.net/store, or through my contact information found at the end of this book. Also, the MP3 audio files are available as free downloads at my website.

About the Author

For over three decades Andrew Wommack has traveled America and the world teaching the truth of the Gospel. His profound revelation of the Word of God is taught with clarity and simplicity, emphasizing God's unconditional love and the balance between grace and faith. He reaches millions of people through the daily *Gospel Truth* radio and television programs, broadcast both domestically and internationally. He founded Charis Bible College in 1994 and has since established CBC extension schools in other major cities of America and around the world. Andrew has produced a library of teaching materials, available in print, audio, and visual formats. And, as it has been from the beginning, his ministry continues to distribute free audiotapes and CDs to those who cannot afford them.

To contact Andrew Wommack please write, email, or call:

Andrew Wommack Ministries, Inc.
P.O. Box 3333 • Colorado Springs, CO 80934-3333
E-mail: awommack@aol.com
Helpline Phone (orders and prayer): (719) 635-1111
Hours: 4:00 AM to 9:00 PM MST

Andrew Wommack Ministries of Europe
P.O. Box 4392 • WS1 9AR Walsall • ENGLAND
E-mail: enquiries@awme.net
UK Helpline Phone (orders and prayer):
011-44-192-247-3300
Hours: 5:30 AM to 4:00 PM GMT

Or visit him on the web at:
www.awmi.net

You've Already Got It!

Have you ever thought, *I'm doing everything I know to do, what's wrong with me? What's it going to take to get God to move on my behalf?* If you have, you're not alone. It's a question most Christians ask and yet remain frustrated with the answers they receive.

The answers usually go something like this: If you will pray a little longer and with more sincerity, spend more time fasting, read a few more chapters in the Bible every day, and quit wasting time in front of the television, then God will answer your prayers. He's just waiting for you to shape up.

In other words, your performance is the problem. The fact is, that couldn't be further from the truth. *You've Already Got It!* is a book filled with the good news that God's response isn't based on the things you must do; it's based on what Jesus did. As you read, you'll gain the knowledge to trust God. It's only the truth you know that will set you free!

Item Code: 1033 6-Tape album

Item Code: 1033-C 6-CD album

ISBN: 1-57794-833-5 Paperback

Is Your Prayer Life Working?

After nearly four decades of ministry, Andrew has asked God many questions about prayer and discovered some important truths through the Scriptures. His prayer life is much different than it was thirty years ago and the results have dramatically improved!

The principles found in this book may not be the only way to pray, but if you are not getting the results your desire, consider changing directions; maybe there is *A Better Way to Pray.*

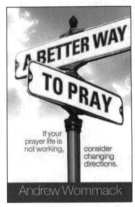

978-1-57794-834-6

Harrison House Publishers
Experience the Power of Charismatic Living!
www.harrisonhouse.com

Other Teachings by Andrew Wommack

Spirit, Soul & Body

Understanding the relationship of your spirit, soul, and body is foundational to your Christian life. You will never truly know how much God loves you or believe what His Word says about you until you do. In this series, learn how they're related and how that knowledge will release the life of your spirit into your body and soul. It may even explain why many things are not working the way you had hoped.

Item Code: 1027 4-Tape album

Item Code: 318-Paperback

Item Code: 1027-C 4-CD album

The True Nature of God

Are you confused about the nature of God? Is He the God of judgment found in the Old Testament, or the God of mercy and grace found in the New Testament? Andrew's revelation on this subject will set you free and give you a confidence in your relationship with God like never before. This is truly nearly-too-good-to-be-true news.

Item Code: 1002 5-Tape album

Item Code: 308-Paperback

Item Code: 1002-C 5-CD album

Living in the Balance of Grace and Faith

This book explains one of the biggest controversies in the church today. Is it grace or faith that releases the power of God? Does God save people in His sovereignty, or does your faith move Him? You may be surprised by the answers as Andrew reveals what the Bible has to say concerning these important questions and more. This will help you receive from God in a greater way and will change the way you relate to Him.

Item Code: 301B-Paperback

The Believer's Authority

Like it or not, every one of us is in a spiritual war. You can't be discharged from service, and ignorance of the battlefield only aids the enemy. In war, God is always for us, and the devil is against us; whichever one we cooperate with will win. And there's only one way the enemy can get your cooperation—and that's through deception. In this teaching, Andrew exposes this war and the enemy for what he is.

Item Code: 1045 6-Tape album

Item Code: 1045-C 6-CD album

Item Code: 1045-D 6-DVD album
(as recorded from television)

The Effects of Praise

Every Christian wants a stronger walk with the Lord. But how do you get there? Many don't know the true power of praise. It's essential. Listen as Andrew teaches biblical truths that will not only spark understanding but will help promote spiritual growth so you will experience victory.

Item Code: 1004 3-Tape album

Item Code: 309-Paperback

Item Code: 1004-C 3-CD album

God Wants You Well

Health is something everyone wants. Billions of dollars are spent each year trying to retain or restore health. So why does religion tell us that God uses sickness to teach us something? It even tries to make us believe that sickness is a blessing. That's just not true. God wants you well!

Item Code: 1036 4-Tape album

Item Code: 1036-C 4-CD album

Fast. Easy.
Convenient.

For the latest Harrison House product information and author news, look no further than your computer. All the details on our powerful, life-changing products are just a click away. New releases, E-mail subscriptions, Podcasts, testimonies, monthly specials—find it all in one place. Visit harrisonhouse.com today!

harrisonhouse

The Harrison House Vision

Proclaiming the truth and the power

Of the Gospel of Jesus Christ

With excellence;

Challenging Christians to

Live victoriously,

Grow spiritually,

Know God intimately.